3000 8000 2
St. Louis Community College

W9-DDW-421

WITHDRAWN

FV

St. Louis Community College

Forest Park
Florissant Valley
Meramec

Instructional Resources
St. Louis, Missouri

The Black Middle Class Family

FAMILY · HOME · INTERACTION

Annie S. Barnes

*"The most significant and thorough study
of the Black family in America
in twenty years."*

*John H. Morgan, Ph.D., D.Sc.(London)
Senior Editor, American Black Studies Library*

 Wyndham Hall Press

LIBRARY
ST. LOUIS COMMUNITY COLLEGE
AT FLORISSANT VALLEY

THE BLACK MIDDLE CLASS FAMILY
A Study of Black Subsociety,
Neighborhood, and Home
In Interaction

Annie S. Barnes
Sociology Department
Norfolk State University

Library of Congress Catalog Card Number

85-051369

ISBN   0-932269-50-8 (paperback)
ISBN   1-55605-087-9 (hardcover)

ALL RIGHTS RESERVED

Copyright © 1985 by Annie S. Barnes

Printed in the United States of America

No portion of this book may be duplicated without the written consent of the author who holds the exclusive copyright. Address inquiries to the author personally or to the publisher: WYNDHAM HALL PRESS, Post Office Box 877, Bristol, IN 46507, U.S.A.

Dedicated to my Husband, Daughter, and Mother

TABLE OF CONTENTS

PREFACE

Over the years the black middle class family has been of interest to social scientists. Starting with E. Franklin Frazier's BLACK BOURGEOISIE in 1957, scholars have provided insight into the black middle class way of life. To contribute to this knowledge, the focus of this study is on the black middle class household and its external relations in the neighborhood and black subsociety. It was enhanced by determining the relationship between the socioeconomic characteristics of the study population and its family behavior. I am, therefore, deeply grateful in general, to the Atlanta black subsociety, as well as to a number of whites, who assisted data collection, and in particular to the residents of Golden towers, a black middle class neighborhood, in northwest Atlanta, Georgia for making this study possible. Certainly, I am also highly appreciative to my doctoral committee, Professors Richard J. Coughlin, Charles Kaut, and Charles Longino, for endorsing and assisting me with the dissertation stage of this project, and to the Ford Foundation and National Science Foundation for grants that made this study possible.

Annie S. Barnes

Norfolk, Virginia

i

CHAPTER ONE

EXPLORATORY FIELDWORK IN ATLANTA, GEORGIA

This study of Black middle class family life in its subsociety, neighborhood, and household was conducted during two field trips. The initial fieldwork was an exploratory study that made an enormous contribution to each stage of the research process. It all began in 1969. During the spring of that year, I reviewed the literature on the black family and black residential areas and wrote several drafts of my dissertation proposal. Though tiring and frustrating, I worked to follow the instructions of my dissertation committee, comprised of Professors Richard J. Coughlin, Charles Kaut, and Charles Longino at the University of Virginia. while I was still working on the proposal, they suggested that I go to Atlanta and conduct an exploratory study to determine whether the project should be attempted in this city. Without delay, I began making appointments with professors at Atlanta University, for I needed a base of operation, as well as assistance with the study. As soon as Professor Richard Long, a former colleague at Hampton Institute in Hampton, Virginia, and now Director of the Center for African and African American Studies at Atlanta University, Professor Clarence A. Bacoate, Chairman of the History Department, and Professor Tillman Cothran, Chairman of the Sociology Department at Atlanta University, my alma mater, gave me appointments, I went to Atlanta. I was deeply appreciative, for my own professors were no longer there. One of them, Professor Hylan Lewis, was then a Professor of Sociology at Brooklyn College, and Professors Mozell Hill and Morris Siegel were deceased. Needless to say, had they been alive, they would have employed their contacts in Atlanta to assist this study.

Though my primary goal was to determine the feasibility of attempting such study in Atlanta, I also desired to rewrite my research proposal and meet a number of people who would help with fieldwork. Essentially, then, I talked with professors at Atlanta University and with a number of people in the Black political, civic, and economic com-

1

munity. The following account of my work shows its nature and procedures, as well as the way social scientists, especially anthropologists, keep a daily journal.

Sunday, June, 8, 1969. Leaving Hampton, Virginia, around midafternoon, I flew to the Atlanta airport and took a limousine to downtown Atlanta, where I took a taxi to Paschal's Hotel in West Atlanta. by the time I got to my room, I was terrified; the only preparation that I could make for the week long project was to sleep.

Monday, June 9, 1969 (My Sixth Wedding Anniversary). I ate breakfast around 8:00 A.M. in the hotel dining room. No sooner than I had finished, I met four Atlanta clergymen: one was a friend of a resident in an Atlanta neighborhood, here called Golden Towers, while another was President of the Interdenominational Theological College in Atlanta. After I returned to my hotel room, around 9:00 A.M., I telephoned Professor Long, who gave me an 11:30 A.M. appointment. Though my breakfast hour had been eventful, I was still terrified about the research experience and wondered what I would say in the interviews. Realizing that I needed a structured interview process, I decided to use it to identify myself, describe the nature of my proposed research, ask the respondents to assess the project, give the names of the most affluent black neighborhoods in Atlanta, and tell whether, in their opinion, this study could be conducted in such settings.

After completing my plan, I went to my luncheon appointment with Long. We talked about anthropology and my research porposal. Essentially, I told him that it focused on the black family and its external relations. Following lunch, we returned to his office. Then he began setting up appointments and requesting help with my project: one appointment was made with Bacoate while another was made with Professor Hubert Ross, one of the first blacks to earn a Ph.D. in anthropology at Columbia University. Once the appointments were confirmed, he advised me to buy a copy of Bacoate's book, THE HISTORY OF ATLANTA UNIVERSITY, and spent two additional hours discussing my research proposal.

When I finished this appointment with Long, I returned to my hotel and, later in the day, I invited two Atlanta women to visit me. One of them, a sister to my daughter's godmother, Ella Harris, knew some of the people who would be involved in this study, including her playmother in Golden Towers. They arrived in the evening, and we spent most of the time talking about Atlanta and the possibility

2

of doing this study in their city. Somewhat late in the evening, I invited them to the Carousel Lounge at Paschal's and, though there was live entertainment, we continued talking about my research. One of the women asked the name of the specific neighborhood that I desired to study. I told her that my preference was Golden Towers, but that such decision ultimately rested with its residents. Before the evening ended, Mary Lowe, sister to our daughter's godmother, pledged her help. Though still very nervous and skeptical about the outcome of this exploratory field trip, I was encouraged by their show of support.

Tuesday, June 10, 1969. Somewhat buoyed by the previous day's activities, I looked forward to eating breakfast in the hotel dining room. It was a great meeting place for blacks of all social classes. What appeared to be the case was that a number of men came to the hotel to eat breakfast, politic, and fellowship and, by 9:00 A.M., the dining room was virtually empty, for the men had gone to the various places of work. This means that most of the breakfast customers were regulars. When a newcomer was in their midst, some one inquired about the person's origin and mission. Such was my case and, therefore, I met a number of Atlanta men. Perhaps, however, the most distinguished Atlantan whom I met today was State Senator Leroy Johnson who, upon my return to Atlanta, helped with my research project.

After another eventful breakfast, I went to a 9:30 a.m. appointment with Bacoate. He was then a twenty-two year resident of Atlanta, who was active in Atlanta politics and its top black social and civic organizations. Though Long confirmed the appointment with Bacoate, as mentioned earlier, before leaving Hampton, I had obtained permission to talk with him. What I have not mentioned, however, is that it was through the assistance of Hylan Lewis, my professor and Masters thesis adviser at Atlanta University and now Professor Emeritus of Brooklyn College, that I initially obtained Bacoate's consent to assist this project. After I explained my research proposal and sought his advice, Bacoate enthusiastically endorsed the project, offered his full support, and referred me to an article, "Some Observations on the Negro Middle Class" by August Meier, reprinted from the October 1, 1957 edition of THE CRISES. Then I asked him to describe the black middle class communities in Atlanta that would be suitable to this study. Bacoate told me that, in West Atlanta, there were four such communities, Collier Heights, Peyton Forest, Cascade Heights, and Hunter-Road Mozley Drive, where the black middle

3

class lived (see Figure 1), and that each community was comprised of several neighborhoods. Then, he suggested that I conduct this study in Golden Towers, a neighborhood in Collier Heights.

To fully lay the ground work for my field research, Bacoate also suggested that I visit Golden Towers and establish contact with at least one of its residents. Before I left his office, he arranged such a visit with Dr. Lois Moreland, a resident of that neighborhood and a professor of Political Science at Spelman College. Because of Bacoate's knowledge of Atlanta and friendship with many of its residents, he made an enormous contribution to this exploratory study. Some of the black Atlanta residents, whom he advised me to see that week, included Mrs. Grace T. Hamilton, a Georgia State Assembly woman and a member of a black first family in Atlanta, Herman Russell, a millionaire, E. B. Williams, Professor of Economics at Morehouse College, Robert Thompson, a thirty-three year resident of Atlanta and an employee of the Atlanta Regional Housing Authority, and B. F. Bullock, an Assistant Professor and Head of Buildings and Grounds at Atlanta University. He was also a member of a black first family in Atlanta and a founder of the Northwest Council of Coordinating Clubs in Collier Heights, discussed in Chapter Four.

By the time that my appointment with Bacoate ended, I felt that the project had a chance of succeeding in Atlanta. However, I continued to meet and talk with as many people as possible. Because I needed at least two weeks to complete my list, I made the decision to talk with those persons who had knowledge directly related to my study; however, after returning to Atlanta in September, 1969, I contacted a majority of the remaining residents on my list.

My next appointment was with Professor Ross who talked with me briefly about my research plans and referred me to the Negro Collection at Atlanta University. He then telephoned his wife and set up a dinner engagement for us and made an appointment for me with Dr. Horace Mann Bond, father of Julian Bond, a black Georgia State Legislator.

As soon as I left this appointment, I went to see Dr. Bond in his home. When I arrived, he was babysitting for two of his granddaughters and combing one's hair. After we met, one of the first things that I did was to ask whether I could brush and braid his granddaughter's hair. He graciously consented and jokingly said, "We are initiating you into your fieldwork." Once we got the children squared away, we turned to my research, and his response was, indeed, gratify-

ATLANTA'S
NEIGHBORHOODS

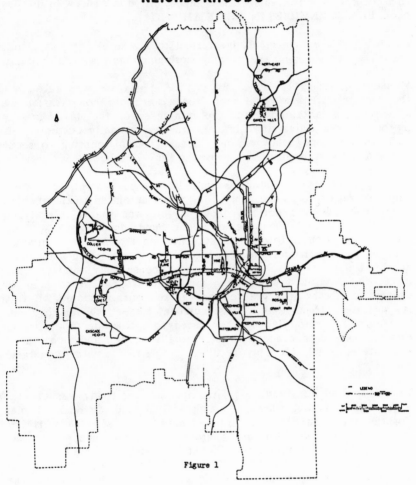

Figure 1

ing. Not only did he endorse it, but he gave me an autographed copy of his latest publication, A STUDY OF FACTORS INVOLVED IN THE IDENTIFICATION AND ENCOURAGEMENT OF UNUSUAL ACADEMIC TALENT AMOUNG UNDERPRIVILEGED POPULATIONS. It traces the geneologies of some blacks who hold doctorates in this country; some of this work is incorporated in Andrew Billingsley's book, BLACK FAMILIES IN WHITE AMERICA.

Following this appointment, I returned to my hotel and was pleased about the day and spent the evening working on my research proposal.

Wednesday, June 11, 1969. By chance, breakfast was eaten with the four ministers whom I met Monday and our conversation was still about Atlanta; however, the remainder of the day was spent in the Atlanta University Library. As was my daily custom, I also went to see Long, who told me that he was attempting to secure a suite for me in faculty housing for the 1969-70 school year.

Since the exploratory study seemingly was successful, thus far, I began to reflect on some other things, not unrelated to the research experience. What I noticed about myself was that I felt strange as well as excited about being among hundreds of black students, interspersed with a few white students, on the Atlanta University campus, the reverse of the scene to which I had grown accustomed at the University of Virginia. Without consciously thinking about it before, I realized that, when time permitted, I stood near the University library and greeted and talked with students. But, to my surprise, I found that a large number of them, though they wore bouffant Afro hairstyles, neither cared to speak nor talk with me. Hence, I sensed that we were not mutually excited about our chance encounters, which probably resulted, in part, from the generation gap.

Thursday, June 12, 1969. My first appointment today was at 11:30 a.m. with Tillman Cothran. Though he endorsed my research plan, Cothran informed me that "the Atlanta black subsociety is hard to crack" and that "the upper group is virtually unapproachable." However, he finally said that it might be possible for me to approach them, but that it would be difficult. He suggested that it would be easier to study a black middle class neighborhood rather than one with a number of upper class blacks. I realized that Cothran was accurate in his prediction, but since this is an anthropological study, I knew that a neighborhood, with a wide range of residents, would prove more valuable than a homogeneous group. Village monographs, for example, usually include a few people, especially chiefs and rich farmers, a cut above the rest of the population, and contribute to the richness of the work. Besides, as far as I have been able to determine, as a rule, black middle class neighborhoods are heterogeneous. As it turned out, Golden Towers was, indeed, a neighborhood comprised of a varied population, including at least one millionaire and two female domestics. It was my opportunity to see one of the domestics chauffered home from work, however, before I began my research, the other domestic had retired. Another reason that I desired to study Golden Towers was because I knew that my status as a student probably gave me the best chance that I would ever have to study such neighborhood; nevertheless, I kept in mind what Cothran had told me and worked hard to remain personna grata.

My next appointment was at 1:45 with B. F. Bullock. He not only endorsed my research plan, but he also gave me an enormous amount of information about the social structure of Collier Heights and a book, by the same name, which greatly enhanced my dissertation proposal.

Starting at 5:00 p.m., I spent forty minutes in the home of Lois Moreland. While we drank coffee and ate pound cake, in the family room, overlooking a grove of trees, Moreland assured me that she would cooperate with the study in the event that Golden Towers was chosen as the research site, but she quickly added, "I will give such help, not because I want to, but for the good of academia." Like Cothran's prediction, she warned me that, "In Atlanta, it is difficult for an outsider to gain access to middle and upper class blacks," which helped me to stay on guard. Moreland, attired in a hostess outfit, was a gracious woman. For example, she stood outside her door and waved goodbye, as I left, a great source of encouragement.

Friday, June 13, 1969. There were the usual talks with Long. Daily conversation with him provided guidance for my exploratory study, encouraged me to spend every available minute in the library, and gave me support. Hence, I spent the remainder of the day reading and writing a new draft of my research proposal.

Saturday, June 14, 1969. I got up around 7:00 a.m. and finished revising my proposal and Long arrived at 12:30 p.m. During our luncheon meeting, he read it and made some changes. When we finished our session, around 2:00 p.m., he carried me to my next

7

appointment, scheduled with Robert Thompson. After the usual explanation of my project, he enthusiastically endorsed it and described Atlanta.

He began by saying that, prior to 1954, Atlanta had thirty four square miles of land, but, in that year, Mayor Hartsfield made a study of Atlantans, particularly the living conditions of blacks, and suggested that eighty seven square miles be added to the City, a plan that was subsequently implemented. Some whites quickly moved into the recently acquired area. About the same time, a large number of blacks began purchasing land and locating lending institutions and builders, which enabled them to also move away from their traditional residential districts. There are several reasons that explain why blacks moved to West Atlanta, Thompson says, including an abundance of land at a relatively low price, the location of black colleges, and the existence of black contractors and black capitalists. The economic assets of black Atlanta, in 1970, Thompson continued, were $75,000,000 to $80,000,000 in the Atlanta Life Insurance Company, $20,000,000 to $25,000,000 at the Citizens Trust Company, and some $9,700 in the Mutual Trust Company. Besides, there were black mortgage companies, such as the Atlanta Banking Company with another $2,500,000 in assets, and the Atlanta black colleges had endowments estimated at some $50,000,000. This economic wealth served as a leverage and caused white lending institutions to make competitive loans, a situation, Thompson says, made Atlanta unique.

Then, Thompson turned to a discussion of Collier Heights and related that "99 percent of the homes were brand new, done by and large with black capital and entrepreneurship." This area is bound on he North by Bankhead, on the South by Collier Road, on the West by Perimeter Road I-285, and on the East by Hightower Road (see Figure 1). He also told me that a number of blacks purchased various tracts of land in Collier Hieghts. One group of black business and professional people, including Dr. J. B. Harris, R. L. Chenault, Geneva Haugabrooks (a Golden Towers resident), Grace T. Hamilton, the Urban League, the late Attorney A. T. Walden, J. P. Whitaker, and the President of the Mutual Savings and Loan Company, for example, bought an eighty five acre tract of land on Sewell Road located on the south side of Gordon Road (see Figure 1). In the same year (1950), Dr. J. B. Harris, "a prominent physician and public-minded citizen," bought fifty two acres of land on the south side of Gordon Road with the idea that both this tract and the preceding one would eventually provide living space for blacks on this side of Gordon Road. Until 1950, Gordon Road was considered the southern boundary between North and South Atlanta. In 1952, the National Development Company, headed by Q. V. Williamson, purchased 375 lots West of Collier Heights, which broke the bottle neck that hindered expansion in Collier Heights.

When Thompson finished discussing Collier Heights, he gave me the following bibliography:

HEARING BEFORE THE UNITED STATES COMMISSION ON CIVIL RIGHTS (Housing) held in Atlanta, Georgia, April 10, 1959, United States Government Printing Office, Washington, D.C.

HOUSING AND MINORITY GROUPS by Robert Thompson and Hylan Lewis, edited by Nathan Glazer and Davis McEntire, University of California Press, Berkeley and Los Angeles, 1960.

THE HANDY MAN OF THE LORD, Reverend J. Williams Borders (The biography of the Pastor of Wheat Street Baptist Church)

Then Thompson turned to the economic role of the black church in Atlanta. he told me, for example, that the Wheat Street Baptist Church, with some 6,000 members, had recently completed a shopping strip and proposed a home, with 150 dwelling units, for the elderly. Another church, Allen Temple (A.M.E.), had sponsored some 221 D-3 units for the elderly. As a footnote to this builidng activity, Thompson informed me that Spelman College was founded in the basement of the Friendship Baptist Church. Perhaps, an appropriate way to end this part of our discussion, Thompson concluded, is to tell you that it was Heman Perry who initiated the real estate business among Atlanta blacks.

According to Thompson, the highest tribute that could be paid to black Atlanta is that it had leadership and money. For example, under the leadership of the National Development Company, the Collier Heights neighborhoods raised approximately $7,500 to finance a land use plan for the orderly growth and development of the Collier Heights area. The Metropolitan Planning Commission supplemented their funds, via services and expertise, to develop such plan. It was later approved by the city government. The plan gave assurance to the home owners that undesirable construction would not be allowed in the area. After more than two hours, Thompson gave me a long list of persons who would assist my study and then carried me back to Paschal's. As soon as we arrived at the hotel, Ross carried me to his home to visit with him and his wife, Edythe, his eleven year old son, Michael, and his daughter, Susan, a college sophomore. While Edythe was preparing supper in their home in Peyton Forest, Professor Ross and their children carried me on a lecture-tour of this community and Cascade Heights.

Upon returning to their home, we enjoyed a delicious dinner of barbecued ribs, turnip greens, and spoon bread. While eating, Dr. Ross and I talked about various anthropologists and the small number of black anthropologists, as well as about his travels and stay in East Africa. We also spent some time talking about what I had learned in Atlanta, a source of considerable support, for I felt at home with the Rosses. This was the beginning of a very fine friendship that I continue to enjoy with them. Sometime after 10:00 p.m., they took me back to my hotel, but not before making plans for the next day.

Sunday, June 15, 1969. By 9:30 a.m., the Ross family had arrived at Paschal's to take me to church with them. It was Father's Day and the Sunday School at the First Congregational Church celebrated it with a Father's Day breakfast. Some 125 persons (forty adults and eighty five children) attended the seated meal. Mrs. Ross and other church women placed bowls of grits, covered with gravy, platters of chicken, and bowls of chicken gravy and rolls on the tables, followed by prayer. While we were eating, Professor Ross informed the people at our table about my research plans, and later introduced me to other members of the church, including Mayor Andrew Young, who invited me to do this study in Atlanta. When I returned in September, the First Congregational church, along with its pastor and Mayor Young's wife, participated in it. As soon as the minister, The Reverend Homer C. McEwen, gave the benediction, Professor Ross carried me to see the exterior of the residence of the late Martin Luther King and to Paschal's. I immediately checked out and took a taxi to the Atlanta airport. At the bottom of these field notes, I wrote (Thanks, Atlanta, for the Magnificent Trip!")

Upon returning home, I visited my dissertation committee at the University of Virginia and received some additional instructions. By the early part of September, they approved my proposal, and I went immediately to Atlanta and, over a ten month period, implemented the plan.

CHAPTER TWO

FIELDWORK

The Research Site and Sample

When I returned to Atlanta in September 1969, for ten months of fieldwork, I was pleased that I had made a number of preliminary plans, including selection of the particular research site, Golden Towers (see Figure 1 in Chapter 1). This neighborhood is located in northwest Atlanta and was begun in 1958 with the settlement of the founder-developer. Since that time, forty additional families have moved to Golden Towers.

These families comprise the neighborhood sample. At the time of this research, seventy one males and ninety one females lived in the neighborhood. However, as shown in Table 1, the largest percentage of the men were between forty and forty-nine years of age while the largest percentage of the women were between thirty and thirty-nine years of age. However, the oldest residents were females, over seventy years of age, and constituted more than 1.2 percent of the population. Judging by age of the adults, it was easy to conclude that considerable variation existed in the ages of children. However, the male children were more nearly the same age, age groups ten to fourteen and thirty to thirty-four excepted, than the female children.

When it comes to the combined income of the Golden Towers spouses, it ranged from the $10,000 to $13,000 category to over $50,000, and the average household income was $25,207.90 in Table 2. As can be seen in Table 3, the residents were employed mainly in white collar occupations; however, eleven adults worked at blue collar jobs, three were in service work, two were retired service workers, and six were housewives. The education of the residents, as shown in Table 4, is also varied; hence, twenty-four of the adults had achieved graduate education, twenty-two had college degrees, and

11

Table 1

Percentage Distribution by Sex and Age
of Household Heads and Spouses
in Golden Towers

Age	Male No.	Male %	Female No.	Female %
70-	7	17.95	15	36.59
60-69	13	33.33	9	21.95
50-59	11	28.21	9	21.95
40-49	8	20.51	6	14.63
30-39	0	0.00	2	4.88
Total	39	100.00	41	100.00

Table 2

Combined Annual Income of Families
in Golden Towers

Class intervals ($)	x Mid-points ($)	f Frequency	fx[a] Calculations ($)
10,000. to 13,999.	11,999.50	4	47,998.00
14,000. to 17,999.	15,999.50	7	111,996.50
18,000. to 21,999.	19,999.50	7	139,996.50
22,000. to 25,999.	23,999.50	2	47,999.00
30,000. to 33,999.	31,999.50	1	31,999.50
50,000. to 100,000.	75,000.00	3	225,000.00
Total		24	604,989.50

[a]x—mid-points times f—frequency equals fx—calculation.

12

Table 3

Occupational Distribution of Husbands
and Wives in Golden Towers

Occupation	Total		Husbands		Wives	
	Num-ber	Per-cent	Num-ber	Per-cent	Num-ber	Per-cent
White collar						
Professional	33	41.25	9	23.08	24	58.54
Clerical	5	6.25	2	5.13	3	7.32
Managers and officials	6	7.50	4	10.26	2	4.88
Proprietors	9	11.25	6	15.38	3	7.32
Clergy	3	3.75	3	7.69		
Sales	1	1.25	1	2.56		
Spiritual consultant	1 .	1.25	1.	2.56		
Blue collar						
Letter carriers	3	3.75	3	7.69		
Craftsmen	6	7.50	6	15.38		
Foremen	2	2.50	2	5.13		
Service workers						
Truck driver	1	1.25	1	2.56		
Domestic worker	2	2.50			2	4.88
Retired service worker	2	2.50	1	2.56	1	2.44
Housewives	6	7.50			6	14.63
Total	80	100.00	39	99.9	41	100.01

Table 4

Educational Distribution by Sex of Household
Heads in Golden Towers

Amount of education completed	Total		Male		Female	
	Num-ber[a]	Per-cent	Num-ber	Per-cent	Num-ber	Per-cent
Graduate school						
Ph.D., M.D., D.D.S., J.D., Pharmaceutical, Science	8	10.0	6	15.4	2	4.9
Master Degree	16	20.0	3	7.7	13	31.7
College						
Four years	22	27.5	7	17.9	15	36.6
One to three years	18	22.5	11	28.2	7	17.1
High school						
Four years	8	10.0	7	17.9	1	2.4
One to three years	2	2.5	1	2.6	1	2.4
Grammar school						
First to eighth grade	6	7.5	4	10.3	2	4.9
Total	80	100.0	39	100.0	41	100.0

[a]Number of cases for whom educational data were secured (two
of the females listed in the Master Degree category have completed
course requirements for the Ph.D. and several in the same category
have six-year teaching certificates).

eighteen had been to college one to three years; eight had high school training, two had one to three years of training, and six had grammar school training. This heterogeneous group was the primary focus of the ten months of field work.

Gaining Entry and Rapport

Though I began this study with a week long trip in June, 1969 and had what seemed to be endless appointments with many distinguished Atlanta citizens, both in the academic and business community, I left Atlanta with mixed feelings. I was, on the one hand, deeply encouraged by the enormous support shown by a large number of my black ethnic group, and on the other hand, I came to the realization quickly that, regardless of common ethnic identity, it would be difficult to develop the intimate ethnographic detail that I wanted on family and neighborhood life. This feeling of uneasiness stayed with me, even after my mother, daughter, and I moved to an apartment in southwest Atlanta to begin my research. In fact, it took a month and half for me to develop enough confidence to attempt to enter the homes in Golden Towers; hence, entry into Golden Towers was a long, drawn out, and frustrating process.

In retrospect, I know that particular sources of frustration were the home settings and delays and interruptions encountered in gaining entry. the formidable appearance of the neighborhood, for example, was more than I had before attempted to enter, which made it difficult to develop enough confidence to enter the neighborhood on my own. This was one reason why I asked the president of the Golden Towers Neighborhood Club to assist my entry and was somewhat encouraged by her reply; "When the neighborhood club meets again, two weeks from now, I will ask them to invite you to the next meeting to explain your project." I waited anxiously to receive her call and, after a month, I inquired about the meeting, only to learn that the club had not set a meeting date. That no one seemed to appreciate my eagerness to get on with my research, that I was so easily kept waiting, was a genuine source of anxiety. This casual use of my time symbolically conveyed the notion that I was not perceived as a member of their social class, for blacks usually give immediate attention to those who are either on their status level or a cut above them.

Other disruptions and delays probably peculiar for that year were sports and political activities. For example, the Atlanta Braves clinched the Western Division title in the National League, and black Atlantans spent more than a week watching the Braves and the New

York Mets compete for the National League Pennant. Immediately after the Braves lost, the October election of city officials was held, followed two weeks later by a run-off election. Nevertheless, after seemingly countless delays and considerable progress with the remainder of my research, I began my neighborhood study.

The Date Collection Process

My data needs in Golden towers can be separated into public versus private types of ethnographic detail. By private data, I refer to personal information concerning the family and its individual members and their relationship to the remainder of the Golden Towers residents while public ethnographic data focus on matters relating to the development of this neighborhood and other residential areas, black realtors and financial institutions, and voluntary associations in the Atlanta black subsociety. The difficulty of inquiry and number of types of research techniques employed varied by type of data sought; furthermore, the status differences between the researcher and the Atlanta residents increased the difficulty of data collection.

The private ethnographic detail included the demographic character-istics of the respondents. Of the selected demographic characteristics sought, only sex of respondents was easy to obtain, and to acquire age data, arbitrary age categories from thirty to thirty-nine to over seventy years of age were established. Even so, two female respon-dents placed themselves in one age category younger than they were, but it is not unusual for blacks to be reluctant to reveal their age; black families, for example, often do not list the age of their deceased relatives in obituary columns. Similarly, blacks, as a rule, consider their annual income a private family matter; hence, to find out the annual income of spouses, income categories were also established. The technique, however, did not ensure total cooperation; in fact, only twenty-four households revealed their annual income category. On the other hand, it was relatively easy to obtain the specific occupa-tions and education achieved, a consequence of pride and difficulty of accomplishment.

Because I realized the problems in collecting select demographic information, I sought to obtain it by mailing a questionnaire and self-addressed and stamped envelope to the respondents which netted almost a fifty percent return. To obtain data on the remainder of the households, I completed the questionnaire with the respondents' help, on the telephone, in their homes, and on their jobs. this procedure required me to telephone them frequently, accept each delay in

16

a congenial manner, and make the next approach to the respondent the same way; thus, with one exception, the data were obtained under agreeable circumstances, but with little regard for my time. Moreover, since the respondents either were not apologetic or only slightly apologetic for the inconvenience and delay they had caused me, I interpreted it to mean they considered my status less important than their own.

Another type of private data sought in Atlanta concerned household interaction with emphasis on spouses. It related to types of authority, conjugal cooperation in the performance of household tasks and its relation to the women's participation in the occupational system, and spouses' affectionate ties. Although the residents talked freely about authority and cooperative conjugal relations, it was impossible to get them to relate the emotional solidarity they had with their spouses; therefore, it was necessary to seek their opinion of the nature of middle class husbands and wife affection and cohesion, as they had observed it.

Parent and child interaction was another type of private data required in this research. In Golden Towers, it was not difficult to obtain parental goals and values for their children, discipline patterns, the relationship between sex of parent, and parent and child emotional bond, children's needs and type of parent and child relationship, the strongest bond in the parent and child behavior complex (Firth,[1] Young and Wollmott,[2] Adam[3]) and stepfather and stepchild relations, but there was some difficulty in determining the nature of disciplining, cooperation, and emotional solidarity in the stepmother and stepchild complex.

The investigation of the influence of age and sex on sibling behavior was the next type of private data investigated. the parents were much more willing to talk about cooperative than antagonistic relations among their children; hence, sibling conflict was somewhat considered a private family matter.

Another type of private data sought related to kinship. The inquiry considered the impact of sex, age, residential status, education, occupation, income, slavery, mixed ancestry, lack of contact, and early death of ancestors on the extent of kin participation, knowledge, and terms of reference. It was relatively easy to research kinship participation, including kin contact, kin assistance, and kin solidarity, and kinship terminology, but, in some cases, genealogical information was the most difficult type of private information to collect, a conse-

17

quence of limited kinship knowledge and sometimes improper birth status of either a respondent or kinsmen. It appeared that both reasons were a source of embarassment to a people who had become social elites. Difficulty in obtaining genealogical data may also be related to the fact that I was an outsider to both their city and social status, and, therefore, since their background was unknown to me, perhaps some residents did not desire to reveal it to one who did not belong. Although a few of the respondents refused to supply genealogical data seemed embarrassed, or chuckled about their kin knowledge, the research situation was cordial.

The neighborly relationship among Golden Towers residents were the next type of private data sought. The inquiry, which focused on the relationship between sex, age, education, occupation, and income and neighborhood participation, including visiting, telephoning, and attending parties with neighbors was difficult to conduct.

The final type of private data sought were daily family rituals and types of household furnishings. The furnishings were considered private only because I desired to see the master bedroom, itemize and categorize each room as either modern, eclectic, or traditional, and they feared that I would report my finding to the government while the rituals were seen as private because they probed the intimate detail of each family member's daily routine.

I utilized several research techniques to assist the collection of data on social interaction, household furnishings and family rituals, including the structural interview. In Golden Towers, it was conducted with thirty-nine of the forty-one households and usually took from three to six hours, divided into two to four visits, but when both spouses participated in the interview, it was likely to be completed in one session. The most difficult problem was obtaining the appointment. A few wives were telephoned fifteen to twenty times before either granting the initial visit or carrying through with the appointment, and usually several telephone calls were made to obtain subsequent visits; the most unusual case was a woman whom I telephoned more than eighty times before she completed the interview, and I was never allowed to obtain her husband's genealogical data. On two occasions, this same wife gave me an appointment and was not at home when I arrived; since she was one of the prestigious women and rarely apologized for the inconvenience she caused, it seemed certain that she neither wanted to reveal certain private family data, nor did she value my time. This type of disappointment was usually averted by telephoning the residents, before leaving my apartment, to remind them of our appointment, which sometimes resulted in its cancellation. Moreover, it was usually difficult to obtain private data from those who had either the highest (physicians, dentists, and Ph.D's) or lowest (service workers) status in the neighborhood than residents who occupied the middle range of prestige; hence, status differences in this middle class neighborhood, in either direction, added to the strain of collecting data. Moreover, some of the residents found it difficult to determine that I was black from our telephone conversations; had a few of them known my race, they would have been less reluctant, they say, to assist the project. Nevertheless, each woman was telephoned, as often as necessary, and delays and conditions were accepted as cordially as appointments, but not without psychological consequences for the researcher. In fact, the research process eroded my self-confidence to the extent that it took three months, after I returned home with my husband, to regain normalcy.

A schedule, based on a procedure employed by Codere[4] among Vassar students, was utilized to collect genealogical data. Similarly, the inventory technique was employed to collect data on household furnishings, and some of the most and least prestigious residents did not allow me to itemize their furnishings. Perhaps the more prestigious residents considered it demeaning to allow their furnishings to be inventoried while it appeared that some of the blue collar residents feared allowing me to write anything about them, including itemization of their furnishings. To handle this problem, I memorized the types of furnishings and decor in each room, went home, as soon as possible, and typed the inventory. On the other hand, only limited difficulty was encountered in the collection of family rituals by utilizing an inventory format.

I found it much more difficult in Atlanta to employ participant observation than the other techniques, genealogical inquiry sometimes excepted, to achieve private data. Although approximately half of the neighborhood allowed me to engage in participant observation, the greater the variation between my status and that of the residents, the more difficulty experienced in obtaining cooperation with participant observation.

The use of informants was the final technique employed to collect private data. There were five women who were either in or slightly below the middle prestige level whom I contacted by telephone or visited and talked informally about particular research questions.

19

These five women were selected to provide in depth assistance, with the research project, because of their congeniality from the beginning of our acquaintance.

Coupled with my effort to remain personna grata, I followed the gift-giving procedure, utilized by anthropologists in non-literate societies, to encourage participation in my research, but I had to decide: (1) to whom gifts should be given, (2) the standards for determining recipients, (3) when gifts should be presented, and (4) the cost and types of gifts. I decided that gifts would be given only to women and children in households that provided one or more opportunities for participant observation and would not be given to particular women who provided participant observation, because it might be considered untactful. Moreover, women were usually given gifts following participant observation while gifts were presented to children upon my arrival and set a congenial tone for participant observation. It was, therefore, easier to give gifts to lower status persons than to higher status individuals. Perhaps, then, it is easier to give gifts down than up the social scale.

Even though an enormous amount of neighborhood cooperation assisted the private data collection phase, six women told me their households would not participate in the research. Of course, this news created more strain than all the previous problems. To get them to congenially reverse their decision, I began immediately to seek assistance in and outside the neighborhood. Mrs. Lottie B. Harris, President of the Women's Auxilliary to the Black Atlanta medical Association and the wife of Dr. J. B. Harris, was one of the three persons, outside Golden Towers, whose assistance was obtained. Since she knew three of the women who had turned down my request, Harris informed them that they were morally obligated to make a contribution to my scholarly endeavor and continued refusal would be an affront to her, because she was personally making the request; consequently, they gave me immediate and friendly assistance. Since two of the women were on the same social level and one was a step below Harris, this situation seems to give proof that members of my ethnic group respond immediately and favorably to those whom they perceive as social equals or superiors.

Unlike the collection of private data, I sought data on meetings and activities of the Golden Towers Neighborhood Club; after several telephone calls, a former president gave me access to all archival records of the organization. Another type of public information sought concerned property in Golden Towers. Once requested, the

20

city gave me immediate access to the Atlanta LAND LOT BOOKS, which provided information on the settlement date, size of lot, assessed tax value of each family's property, and number of times it had changed ownership. Visual records of Golden Towers families, the setting in which household and neighborhood behavior takes place, and voluntary association activities in the Atlanta black subsociety were also sought.

Public data were also sought on the first black settlers in Atlanta, demography, migration, and the nature of the Coordinating Council of Northwest clubs, the Atlanta Chapter of Jack and Jill of America, the First Congregational and Mount Zion Second Baptist Churches, and black traditional and modern residential patterns. In a relatively short time, I utilized a variety of research techniques, including the structured interview, questionnaire, and participant observation, and archives to obtain all the public data needed.

Although my research experiences in Atlanta were difficult, the residents allowed me to maintain the image of an anthropologist. They did not attempt to get me to share the data I had obtained, with one exception, nor was there any indication that they expected the research to improve their circumstances. Moreover, although I "assumed the inside view,"[5] I did not become a member of the Atlanta black middle class, for I was both an outsider to their city and social class. In my opinion, it would have taken at least several years for me to develop acceptable trappings to become a member of the Atlanta black middle class.

Since I had been in Golden Towers for a considerable amount of time, by spring, my research efforts needed a boost. About that time, Professor Richard Coughlin wrote that he would soon attend the meeting of the Southern Sociological Society in Atlanta, and that he planned to visit my research site. Because I knew that my entire dissertation committee was interested in my work, because I knew that such a visit would cause the families to have renewed interest in my research, when I learned that he would soon join me in the field, I was ecstatic. After he arrived at the conference site, I met him at the hotel conference site, took him to Paschal's for dinner and to my apartment to meet my mother and daughter and to see the mounds of notes that I had typed and organized in huge notebooks. We also visited a variety of families and saw a wide range of house types that gave Professor Coughlin a feel for the neighborhood. Just as I had expected, the families considered it a fine gesture for my professor to be interested enough in my research to obtain first hand knowledge about the research site and process. This, of course, does not mean that there were no other delays, however, it does mean that this visit served to help guarantee that the research process would be completed by my specifications and, indeed, that is what happened.

Conclusions

That status diferences between anthropologists and her/his subjects influence the research process is evident in the foregoing account. In summary, the effects may be stated in the following ways. First, the socioeconomic status of the group influenced the level of difficulty experienced in obtaining private data; hence, the higher the socioeconomic status of the family, the more difficult it was to obtain their participation in the family and neighborhood components.

Second, when the anthropologist's socioeconomic status is lower than that of his subjects, the role of researcher is fraught with strain. In Atlanta, for example, during the preliminary phase of my research, I realized enormous tension while anticipating the outcome of my conferences with Atlanta residents concerning the nature and feasibility of conducting my research plan.

Third, strain was also experienced while gaining entry to the research sites. I experienced a great deal of anxiety, during the month and a half I attempted to gain enough confidence to enter Golden towers, a neighborhood more formidable than I had before witnessed, and waited for the neighborhood club to meet and approve my research plan, and the proper timing to approach the residents. A related source of strain concerns the permanence of entry. It was always precarious and contingent upon appropriate deference to the research population.

Fourth, a great deal of strain was also experienced in Atlanta during the data collection process. The research process was fraught with frustration, because I conducted it almost single handed and trust in my confidentiality had to be developed. Another source of strain in the data collection process was the casual use of my time. The Atlanta residents required me to utilize hundreds of hours telephoning for appointments and confirming them in subsequent calls to avoid disappointment. When the data collection process ended, I had learned much and loved the participants beyond my fondest imaginations, yet I felt like a non-person. Furthermore, in Atlanta, strain was enhanced by the need to employ several research techniques to collect a single type of data; for example, demographic data were achieved through mailing questionnaires and receiving some of them back in the mail, telephoning for appointments to complete the remainder of the questionnaires, and completing them in interviews or on the telephone, in their homes, and on their jobs.

Fifth, another type of strain in the research process concerns the collection of certain types of data. I did not find it possible to obtain husband wife demographic and emotional specific data in Atlanta. Moreover, difficulty was encountered in Atlanta in obtaining names of neighborhood friends and party guests, particular types of neighborhood behavior, an itemized account of household furnishings, genealogical information, and opportunities to engage in participant observation.

Sixth, gift giving was another source of strain in the research process. It was easier to give gifts to lower status persons than to higher status persons. Additionally, it was necessary to present gifts, when utilizing the most difficult research technique, which was participant observation. It was, therefore, arduous to mingle with members of my ethnic group.

Seventh, status differences made it necessary for the researcher to manifest a malleable personality. Although I was rarely inconvenienced in the city and black subsociety in Atlanta, the difficulty of obtaining appointments and somewhat frequent cancellations in Golden Towers required frequent and congenial adjustments. The constancy of such experiences eroded my self-confidence that was regained only after leaving the field.

Eighth, common ethnic identity, marital status, my husband's monthly visits, and the presence of my daughter and mother in Atlanta contributed to the quality of data received. Although the residents did not supply specific demographic data, I was able to study, in depth, and obtain accurate data about many life ways, that had not been studied among blacks, because I am black and married. Moreover, a few residents only participated in the study because of my race and still others were made to feel obligated to assist a member of their ethnic group.

Ninth, status differences inhibited the anthropologist from being coopted by her research group. The Atlanta residents allowed me to maintain the image of an anthropologist, and they did not make any request of me for the future.

That is was difficult to conduct this fieldwork in Atlanta is evident in this essay. Nevertheless, I am grateful that the Atlanta citizens, and the Golden Towers residents, in particular, contributed generously to this ethnographic report about the black family in its home, neighborhood, black subsociety, and residential areas.

NOTES

1. Raymond Firth. TWO STUDIES OF KINSHIP IN LONDON. London: Athlone Press, 1956, p. 63.

2. Michael Young and Peter Willmott. FAMILY AND KINSHIP IN EAST LONDON. London: Routledge and Kegan Paul, 1957, p. 157.

3. Bert N. Adams. KINSHIP IN AN URBAN SETTING. Chicago: Markham Publishing Company, 1968, p. 169.

4. Helen codere. "A Genealogical Study of Kinship in the United States," PSYCHIATRY xviii (1955), pp. 65-79.

5. Robert Redfield. THE LITTLE COMMUNITY AND PEASANT SOCIETY AND CULTURE. Chicago: The University of Chicago Press, 1956, p. 82.

CHAPTER THREE

NEGRO RESIDENTIAL PATTERNS IN ATLANTA, GEORGIA,

1860-1983, AND THEIR IMPACT ON PUBLIC SCHOOL MIXING

Social scientists have long been aware of the importance of the city and its residential areas as a unit of research. As early as the 1920's , they focused on such ecological processes as invasion,[1] succession,[2] and segregation[3] in residential areas. The United States Commission on Civil Rights considers the real estate broker the "key man in the majority of housing transactions," and segregation as the rule rather than the exception.[4] Similarly, Darden, based on data collected between 1959 and 1970, found that real estate brokers, owners of dwellings, financial institutions, newspapers, and home-builders, in that order, influence residential segregation in Pittsburgh.[5] Although Darden devotes only about a page to his discussion of Negro brokers, he concludes that "black real-estate brokers have become the most powerful anti-discriminatory force in Pittsburgh."[6] And though Hartshorne discusses Negro residential expansion between 1950 and 1970, there is no mention of Negro real estate brokers,[7] but Thompson et al., in their study of Negro housing in Atlanta and Birmingham, give Heman Perry credit for being the pioneer Negro real estate broker in Atlanta.[8] To expand the perspective of Negro realtors, this article determines whether the enterprising efforts of Negro real estate brokers and Negro financiers figured significantly in Negro residential settlement and expansion, in Atlanta, Georgia, from 1860 to 1983, and the relationship between residential patterns and public school mixing. Similar to earlier studies, a key concept in this study is invasion. It is conceptualized as a complex physical, emotional, economic, political, and social process used to acquire housing for Negroes. Another key concept in this article is blockbust-

Reprinted by permission from Volume 21, Numbers 1-6 of INTEGRAT-EDUCATION, published by the Horace Mann Bond Center for Equal Education, University of Massachusetts, Amherst.

ing, a process whereby Negro brokers buy property in white residential neighborhoods and move a Negro family, who may or may not pay rent, into the home. Once it becomes known, white neighbors immediately put For Sale signs on their property. As soon as Negroes move into an area, whites help sell the remainder of the homes and sometimes make more money than Negroes who initiated the process. Of course, up until 1975, Negro brokers in Atlanta took the lead in obtaining housing for Negroes, but in 1975, there was a recession and realtors were among the first to feel its impact. It has thus been difficult, since that time, for realtors, especially Negroes, to help clients obtain loans, which means that, recently, white brokers have sold more homes than Negro brokers to Negro clients. Regardless of the real estate group that has taken the lead in selling homes to Negroes, their neighborhoods, in 1983, have fewer whites than the same neighborhoods had in 1970.

After a few Negroes move into a neighborhood, the next ecological process is succession and, in Atlanta, it means that newly acquired areas quickly become predominantly Black, sometimes against the desires of new occupants. What this suggests, is that succession is sometimes a process that is met with resistance from Negro and white neighbors. And when another key concept, Negro real estate brokers, is employed in this study, it refers to Negro male real estate company owners and salesmen who initiated expansion in such West Atlanta areas as Ashby Street, Hunter Street and Mozley Park, Collier Heights, Peyton Forest, and Cascade Heights. The final major concept, Negro financiers, in this article, refers to three Negro financial lending institutions, the Atlanta Life Insurance Company ($75,000,000 to $80,000,000), the Citizens and Trust Bank ($20,000,000 to $25,000,000), and the Mutual Savings and Loan Association (approximately $10,000), that were "prime movers of Negro expansion in West Atlanta," the brokers say. And, as these 1970 assets suggest, Atlanta is different than Pittsburgh where "only one Black owned and operated financial institution (2.9,000,000) engaged in mortgage lending."[9] This article, therefore, deals with the same concepts found in other research, but from a somewhat different perspective.

Method.

The majority of the data for this chapter was collected in Atlanta, Georgia between September 1969 and August 1970, as part of a larger study about Negro life. Various methods of data collection, such as touring Negro neighborhoods and studying maps, were utilized to collect this information. Interviews with Atlanta residents of both races, Negro real estate brokers who helped expand Negro communities, and with an engineer in city Hall were also employed to obtain information about Negro residential settlement and expansion in Atlanta. These 1970 data were updated January 1983, by obtaining maps and information from the Atlanta Bureau of Planning and Information and statistics from Q. V. Williamson, a long-time Atlanta realtor, who participated in my original study of Atlanta, and from the Statistics Department of the Atlanta School Administration Office. After the interview information had been written and/or put in tabular form, I telephoned, again, the interviewees, to check its accuracy. This chapter, therefore, focuses on Atlanta Negro residential patterns and expansion from 1860 to 1983 and their impact on school mixing in 1970 and 1983.

Traditional Black Residential Neighborhoods.

The settlement of Negroes in Atlanta dates back to the end of the first quarter of the nineteenth century. It was in the year 1825, four years after the origin of Atlanta, that Negroes were known to be in this city. They were slaves of the Atlanta Cherokee Indians and servants for whites, and a few of them were free, but there were no Negro settlements.[10] As noted in Figure 1, Chapter 1, since that time, Negroes have occupied a number of residential areas, including Vine City.

Vine City.

Starting in the 1980's, a large number of Negro migrants moved from the plantation to Atlanta. Vine City, situated on low and elevated land Northwest of the Central Business District (CBD) where whites also lived, was settled initially, in 1865, and received its name from one of its streets, Vine Street. This name for the area has come into use only since World War II; prior to that time, it was known as "the area back of the railroad terminal." Since the area was settled by both races, it is likely that the major concern focused on getting loans, a problem that Negroes faced during the first 40 years of this century.

Buttermilk Bottom.

As early as 1865, Negroes began to occupy another area in Atlanta, known as Buttermilk Bottom. It is a low land area, South of the CBD and was known originally as the Butler Street Bottom. Unlike Vine City, as a result of urban renewal, this is mainly the location for several commercial institutions, including the Atlanta Civic Center and parking facilities. What happened in Atlanta, is that between 1956 and 1965, low income housing construction (4,000 units) lagged behind the needs of the poor families and the growing black population; in fact, slum clearance and highway construction in Atlanta resulted in additional crowding of Negroes in the ghettos.[11]

Summerhill.

Summerhill, an elevated community, located Southeast of the CBD is another traditional Negro neighborhood in Atlanta and it, too, dates back to 1865. Though there was no interracial visiting, between its settlement and 1970, Summerhill was occupied by Negroes and whites, which made invasion and succession unnecessary. Though both races occupied the community, judging by the fact that some three or four years after slavery, the early settlers asked that their residential area be named after a Negro, Armstrong Walker Bailey,[12] it appears that Negroes enjoyed a rather high status in this neighborhood. Bailey, however, declined the offer and, instead, named it Summerhill.

Peoplestown.

Peoplestown, developed Southwest of the CBD, was another community begun in 1865. Just as Negroes and whites lived in Vine City and Summerhill, until 1960, both races occupied this neighborhood. Residential segregation, however, was evident in the community, for, originally, whites lived on high land on both ends of Peoplestown, while Negroes lived in between on low land, separated from them by a lumber yard at one end and a street on the other end. Though residential segregation existed in Peoplestown, succession was not seen there until almost a hundred years after its origin, and invasion, and the real estate broker was unrelated to expansion in Peoplestown.

The Atlanta University Center.

Negroes continued to expand in Atlanta and, in 1867, the area around Atlanta University, a predominantly Negro graduate institution, was settled on the Southwest side of the CBD on an elevated site. Such development came about largely due to the influence of Edmund Asa Ware, a superintendent of schools for the American Missionary Association.[13] Since that time, Atlanta University and Clark (1877), Morehouse (1879), Morris Brown (1885) and Spellman (1888) colleges have become the Atlanta University Center.

Pittsburgh and Mechanicsville.

Pittsburgh and Mechanicsville were the last traditionally Negro neighborhoods developed. Pittsburgh is situated on both low and elevated land South of the CBD and came into existence in 1880. The smoke from the locomotives and repair shops made the area smoky, resembling Pittsburgh, Pennsylvania; hence, the origin of its name. Mechanicsville, an elevated site, which is also located South of the CBD, has existed only since 1940. In Pittsburgh and Mechanicsville, whites and Negroes, until the 1960's, lived on the same streets, and families of both races visited inside each others' homes and sat in each others' yards, and their children played together. Unlike other settlements, residential segregation was not noticable, nor were invasion and succession utilized to obtain the residential districts.

The Role of Negro Brokers.

Now the question is what was the role of Negro real estate brokers in the six traditional residential areas. Antoine Graves, says Lottie B. Harris, his daughter, who is also the granddaughter of Armstrong Bailey, and the wife of a prominent Atlanta physician, John B. Harris, was "the first Colored real estate agent in Atlanta, and his clients were rich white families who thought no one in Atlanta knew the business like him." Nevertheless, prior to the 1920's, there were also some Negro brokers who sold homes in the traditional residential areas and in some other communities, long before the last two of the six traditional areas were settled.

West Atlanta.

Starting around 1846, the Negro realtors say, Atlanta was planned for whites, evident by a transportation system and utility services, such as sewerage, water, and gas, developed only in the white community, while Negroes used outdoor toilets and wells and provided their own transportation to work, unless, of course, domestics were chauffered to work. Writing in 1977, Clark shows that Atlanta, at that time, still had not built an integrated and comprehensive transportation system, though such was the aim of the Metropolitan Atlanta Rapid Transit Authority (MARTA).[14] It now appears that its rapid rail system, whose trains travel some 60 miles an hour, is fast approaching its goal. The system is comprised of an East-West Line that starts in Avondale, in DeKalb County, and extends to Hightower West and a North-South Line that now extends from 15th

Street and Peachtree Street in the north to West End in the South, but only the East-West Line has been completed. The MARTA system is not only comprised of a rail project, but it also includes a number of feeder buses that circulate in neighborhoods and carry residents to the nearest MARTA station. Since a large number of Atlanta Negroes live on the west side of Atlanta, these findings suggest they have cleared the hurdle of inadequate public transportation. Though it has often been inadequate, Negro expansion has moved according to the way they progessed economically, one realtor says.

Ashby Street.

The first significant expansion in West Atlanta began on Ashby Street in the 1920's. But it was Heman Perry, a Negro man from St. Louis, who came to this city and developed the Standard Life Insurance Company and the Service Realty Company who initiated the movement. The realty company bought and sold homes on Ashby Street, where whites were moving out and, between 1922 and 1924, it obtained, on Ashby Street, 300 acres of land, for $30,000 and built some 511 homes. The city purchased 40 of the 300 acres of land along Ashby Street, from the Service Realty Company, at a cost of $40,000. Such profit caused the Service Realty Company's board of directors to jump on top of the conference table and cheer, but their lack of experience in making and obtaining loans caused the company to go bankrupt. Nevertheless, the Negro real estate broker had begun to take a major role in determining land usage in Atlanta and Negro westward expansion had begun on Ashby Street, in segregated neighborhoods, through invasion and succession.

Hunter Street and Mozley Drive and Park Area (Martin Luther King, Junior Drive).

Both of these streets, located in West Atlanta, three miles from the Central business District, are now known as Martin Luther King, Junior Drive and represent Negroes' second major move from their traditional neighborhoods. As they expanded, the Hunter section of the street was extended, for whites would not live on the same street with them. Whites lived on the other end of this street, called Mozley Drive. It was not uncommon in Atlanta, for a street, occupied by both races, to have two different names and sometimes, the two sections, such as Simpson Road and Collier Drive, were separated only by a traffic light. The expansion process in the Hunter Street-Mozley Drive area was largely under the control of the Empire Real

Estate board, organized in 1935, to provide Negro realtors membership in a real estate organization.

Expansion into the Hunter Street and Mozley Drive area began in 1949, when John Calhoun, a member of the Board, found 10 to 12 unoccupied lots on Hunter Street and listed the homes of three white women for sale. The sale of two of the homes caused a great deal of concern on that street and throughout Atlanta and some Klan activity. As a result, Calhoun was arrested, stood trial, and though his case was declared a mistrial, the Georgia Real Estate Commission revoked his license. It was finally resolved when the members of the Empire Real Estate Board initiated a court case that reinstated the realtor.

While Calhoun continued to sell homes and wait for his trial, the Empire Real Estate Board developed a strategy to obtain Mozley Drive. It required them to obtain housing for Negroes in all white areas surrounding Mozley Drive by assigning the job to four realty companies. One company would, therefore, sell homes on Chicamauga Street, located east of Mozley Drive, while another company would sell homes on Westview Drive, south of Mozley Drive. Then, a third company would sell homes in Mozley Park, north of Mozley Drive, while still a fourth company would sell homes in West Lake, located west of Mozley Drive. In the meantime, a white resident called J. A. Arnold, a Negro realtor, and told him that 14 of them wanted to sell their homes to Negroes. That turn of events opened up Mozley Park and later Mozley Drive, but the sale of homes, initially, was made possible by loans from the Negro financial institutions.

Collier Heights.

The third major move of Atlanta Negroes from their traditional neighborhood was to Collier Heights, a Northwest Atlanta residential area. It all began in 1952 when Q. V. Williamson, a Negro Broker, was looking for a two-acre lot to build a home. As it turned out, he was unable to find one that fitted his plans. But sometime later, in the same year, he found a two-hundred acre tract of land where a white developer, starting in 1945, had begun to "cut streets" and lots, but only 25 percent of the lots had been sold to whites who had not yet built homes. He and a number of other Negroes formed the National Development Company, and bought the tract of land. Whites, however, had begun to construct homes in an adjacent area, and when they learned about the purchases, they sent a committee to ask the head of the company, Williamson, why they bought the

31

land. Upon finding the Negroes planned to develop a residential neighborhood, they proposed separate streets for Negroes and whites, or the construction of a buffer zone or an expressway. Since the company found the racial zoning proposals unacceptable, the whites sold their homes and moved to other locations. Though they paid only $4,000 to $6,000 for their homes, they sold them to Negroes for $8,000 to $10,000, but on the piece of land that abuts this neighborhood, the development company built larger homes that cost between $22,000 and $60,000.

Peyton Forest and Cascade Heights.

The fourth move from traditionally Negro areas occurred in 1962, 10 years after the acquisition of Collier Heights. It began when J. A. Alston and M. H. Callaway, real estate brokers, unexpectedly, found 10 new and unsold homes in Peyton Forest, an upper middle class white southwest Atlanta residential section. They used a number of tactics to obtain their homes, such as asking owners to list their homes with their agencies and attempting to convince homeowners, in two meetings, to sell their homes to Negroes. Though both attempts failed, a white resident who was in financial difficulty, sold his home to a Negro doctor. When this happened, the Atlanta mayor "literally blocked off Peyton Road with no pretense at any motivation other than to prevent further Negro expansion on Peyton Road."[15] Nevertheless, the wall was soon dismantled and the entire area was opened for sale to Negroes.

Though Negro brokers opened the neighborhood, two white real estate brokers, who lived in Peyton Forest, sold most of the homes. Negro brokers who sold some of the homes, often received their clients from white realtors. What sometimes happened was that a Negro client went to a white broker and asked for a home in Peyton Forest. The broker then referred the client to a Negro broker who sold the home and "split the profit" with his white "Real Estate Buddy," Negro brokers say. The invasion process was made possible by the Atlanta Life Insurance Company, which financed all the homes sold to Negroes in Peyton Forest." Nevertheless, this was "the last time that Negroes had to fight for good housing in Atlanta."

Cascade Heights, located next to Peyton Forest, was the fifth major move of Negroes from their traditional residential areas. Unlike Peyton Forest, it was opened in a few weeks, without incident, but the real estate transactions were handled almost entirely by white brokers. The Negro brokers thought that Cascade Heights was their turf, but to their surprise, most of the homes were sold by white brokers "who made good money in the area." They were unsuccessful, for they told white homeowners, "List your homes with us, because Negroes cannot sell to Negroes."

When Negroes expanded to West Atlanta, whites fled to the suburbs. This process helps support the Griers' prediction that by the year 2000, it is likely that there will be "Negro majorities in the core cities of most of the nation's metropolitan areas."[16] In fact, 66.6 percent of 283,000 of the 425,000 Atlanta residents, in 1980, were Black while 6,000 were Spanish and 136,000 were white.

Impact of Residential Segregation on School Board Integration.

Black residential expansion into formerly white neighborhoods has not contributed significantly to racial school mixing. This finding is supported by Berry and Horton who state that "middle-class white families tend to leave their previously stable neighborhoods for homes in more homogeneous school-attendance areas."[17] This is a great disappointment to Negro residents in such neighborhoods as Peyton Forest and Cascade Heights. It was put this way, by a college professor in Peyton Forest, "We moved here so that our children could attend an integrated school and, once some of us moved to the community, we told the rest of the whites they did not have to sell their homes, but most of them moved out, and we are now thinking about sending our children to private schools." It thus appears that some Atlanta Negroes who attempted to use integrated neighborhoods to give their children an opportunity to attend integrated schools must find other and more expensive means of achieving such goals and that many whites neither desire integrated neighborhoods nor integrated schools.

The extent of school segregation is more vivid in 1983 than in 1970, as seen in the elementary schools. Though the Collier Elementary School in Collier Heights was totally segregated in 1970 as well as in 1983, the Cascade Elementary School in Cascade Heights was predominantly white in 1970, but it is almost totally Black in 1983 and Peyton Elementary School in Peyton Forest has only two white students today, compared with its seven white students in 1970. Another factor is that the enrollment has declined at Cascade and Peyton Elementary Schools, formerly white schools, while it has increased at Collier Elementary School, a traditionally Black school. These findings are supported by Berry et. al. who stated, "The continuing white exodus is revealed clearly enough in the racial headcounts in the public elementary schools and the public high schools."[18]

The extent of school segregation, throughout the city, is seen in the Atlanta School Administration Office data. It shows that in 1983, there were 68,492 children in the public school system. Of this number 62,693 were Black, 5,203 were white, 309 were Spanish and 341 belonged to the "Other" category. What this means is that all the public schools in Atlanta are predominantly Black except Northside on Northside Drive in north Atlanta, North Fulton on North Fulton Drive in northeast Atlanta, and Roosevelt on Rosalia Street in southeast Atlanta. Northside and North Fulton are about 50 percent Black and 50 percent white, while Roosevelt has a few more Black than white students. And all the Atlanta elementary schools are predominantly Black, except Sarah Smith on Old Ivy Road in northeast Atlanta and Margaret Mitchell on Margaret Mitchell Drive in northwest Atlanta, where the school population is about evenly divided between the races. Perhaps it should also be stated that the greatest school mixing is in north Atlanta, where some of the wealthiest whites live and in a southeast Atlanta neighborhood where less affluent residents live.

Implications of Findings.

These findings suggest a number of things, including the fact that Atlanta Black residential districts are more segregated in 1983 than in 1970 and 1960, and that public schools are more segregated now than in 1970. They also suggest that Blacks desire to live in mixed neighborhoods and send their children to mixed schools while some whites resist residential mixing and that school segregation reflects residential segregation. Another implication is that the Atlanta Student Voluntary Transfer Program is relatively ineffective, but it indicates that some Black children are willing to be bused to school. A larger implication of these findings is that, initially, whites did not leave Atlanta because of busing. Instead, they left because Black realtors pressured or asked them to sell their homes to Blacks and because they did not want Blacks as their neighbors. Besides, as was shown in the discussion of Collier Heights, whites received enormous profit from sale of their homes to Blacks, and it is likely that the profit motive also influenced movement to suburbs.

These findings seem to suggest that the view, heard in Southern cities, that busing causes parents to move to the suburbs, may not be accurate. Since busing children to school is an old American tradition, for both whites and Blacks, it is odd that busing children to school has caused a great deal of controversy. Prior to the 60's, Black high school children were bused up to 24 miles, each way, to school, though some of them were in walking distance of white high schools that could be called their neighborhood schools and elementary children (first through sixth grade) were bused up to 10 miles, each way, to school. Besides, a number of Black high school students walked several miles, each way, to school. What this means is that it is alright to allow students to tire themselves out walking to school and to have neighborhood schools and go elsewhere to maintain segregation, but that it is wrong, so to speak, to bus students for the purpose of integrating them in a productive learning experience. Perhaps if this inconsistency is eliminated, America will move forward with a busing program that is the only way to give all children equal educational opportunities. For most Negroes, their frequent deficiencies of background and home environment, need to be leavened through contact with more fortunate children.[19]

These findings in Atlanta suggest that racial mixing in the three high schools and two elementary schools is, indeed, an ideal type of school situation for a country well known for using cheap and free Negro labor in its development. It is illustrated in the following advertisement that appeared in the ATLANTA 'NTELLIGENCER, May 11, 1864.[20]

Robert A. Crawford
(Formerly Crawford, Frazer & Co.)
NEGRO DEALER
Peachtree Street, Atlanta, Georgia
The most expensive Negro depot in the Confederacy,
clean, healthy, safe, and comfortable.
Porters experienced and trusty lock-up
Discipline and fare, all right.
STOCK CONSTANTLY REPLENISHED
usually on hand
cooks (meat and Pastry), washers and ironers,
house servants, and seamstresses, blacksmiths,
carpenters, field hands, shoemakers,
plow boys and girls, body servants, waiters,
drivers and families.
My extensive acquaintance and long experience in
the business secure speedy and satisfactory sales.
Parties sending me Negroes by Railroad will find
my old and trusty Porters, "Andrew" and
"Anthony," about the train as usual.

Robert A. Crawford
No. 10 Peachtree Street

As implied in this advertisement, an acre and a mule are no longer adequate. Every Negro child needs high quality education, in integrated schools, with people who will give them exposure to new ways of life and help them prepare for effective functioning in the integrated labor market. In other words, Negro children need a consistent experience in the American society that includes interaction with different races and social classes. Atlanta is an ideal place to start giving back to Negroes what they have given this country.

§§§§§

NOTES

1. Morton Grodzins. THE METROPOLITAN AREA AS A RACIAL PROBLEM. Pittsburgh: University of Pittsburgh Press, 1958, p. 6.

2. **Ibid.**

3. Charles Tilly et al. RACE AND RESIDENCE IN WILMINGTON, DELAWARE. New York: Columbia University Press, 1965, p. 50.

4. United States Civil Rights Commission. HOUSING. Washington: Government Printing Office, 1961, pp. 122-123.

5. Joe T. Darden. AFRO-AMERICANS IN PITTSBURGH. Lexington: D. C. Heath and Company, 1973, p. 42.

6. **Ibid.** p. 55.

7. Truman A. Hartshorne. METROPOLIS IN GEORGIA: ATLANTA'S RISE AS A MAJOR TRANSACTION CENTER. Cambridge: Ballinger Publishing Company, 1976, pp. 46-51.

8. Robert A. Thompson et al. STUDIES IN HOUSING AND MINORITY GROUPS. Berkely and Los Angeles: University of California Press, 1960, pp. 19, 28.

9. Joe T. Darden. AFRO-AMERICANS IN PITTSBURGH. op. cit., p. 55.

10. Franklin M. Garrett. ATLANTA AND ITS ENVIRONS Vol 1. New York: Lewis Historical Publishing Company, 1954, p. 73.

11. Samuel L. Adams. BLUEPRINT FOR SEGREGATION: A SURVEY OF ATLANTA HOUSING. Atlanta: The City of Atlanta, 1967, p. 12.

12. Allen Temple African Methodist Church. EXCERPT HISTORY. Atlanta: Allen Temple African Methodist Church, 1968, p. 1.

13. Clarence Bacoate. THE STORY OF ATLANTA UNIVERSITY. Princeton: Princeton University Press, 1969, pp. 6,7.

14. Johnnie L. Clark. "Planning, MARTA, and the City's Future Direction - A Response." In Edwin N. Gorsuch and Dudley S. Hines (eds.) THE FUTURE OF ATLANTA'S CENTRAL CITY, 1977, p. 47.

15. Samuel L. Adams. BLUEPRINT FOR SEGREGATION: A SURVEY OF ATLANTA HOUSING, op. cit., p. 6.

16. George and Eunice Grier. EQUALITY AND BEYOND. Chicago: Quadrangle Books, 1966, p. 14.

17. Brian J. L., Berry and Frank E. Horton. GEOGRAPHIC PERSPECTIVES ON URBAN SYSTEMS. Englewood Cliffs: Prentice Hall, Inc., 1970, p. 413.

18. Brian J. L. Berry and I. Cutler. CHICAGO: TRANSFORMATIONS OF AN URBAN SYSTEM. Ballinger Publishing Company, 1976, pp. 61-62.

19. Grier and Grier. EQUALITY AND BEYOND. op. cit., p. 42.

20. Franklin M. Garrett. "Atlanta and Environs." THE ATLANTA HISTORICAL BULLETIN, XIV, 4, December 1969, p. 107.

CHAPTER FOUR

THE BLACK SUBSOCIETY

As suggested in Chapter 3, blacks in Atlanta tend to live among members of their subsociety. It is conceptualized here as the setting in which most of the behavior of blacks takes place. Realizing there is a relatively large number of blacks in religious, social, and civic organizations, I studied two churches, several social groups, and a civic organization in Atlanta to describe its black subsociety.

Black voluntary association participation is conceptualized as special interest groups[1] that accord prestige, decision making power,[2] and self-expression. This essay describes and compares the functions of religious and social organizations, along with a civic organization, and their significance, for the effective adaptation of blacks in Atlanta. The social organizations focus on recreation and the churches emphasize religious worship while the civic groups concentrate on community protection. Nevertheless, the identification of groups as social, religious, and civic merely denotes their primary goals and not their total perspective; hence, all groups share common characteristics.

The origin of voluntary association participation in the black subsociety is in the church and goes back to the time of slavery. At that time, there were slave owners who required blacks to participate in their church services while some owners permitted black preachers to conduct church meetings, and a few slaves held secret church services in their homes. To prevent detection, an iron wash pot, an Atlanta resident says, was turned upside down outside the door of the meeting place to absorb the sounds.

The church "is the only social institution of Negroes which started in the African forest and survived slavery,"[3] and the oppression and limited opportunities of the slavery era enhanced its significance[4] Even today, the church is still "the most pervasive community social organization in six Negro communities in Tampa, Florida";[5] moreover, according to a national survey, 83 percent of the black population attends church at least once a month and nearly half of them attend church at least twice a month.[6] In Golden Towers, the residents had attended Sunday School and church since childhood but only a few families now attend Sunday School. However, in eighteen of the forty-one households, all the children and/or husbands and wives attended church and, in the remainder of the households, at least one person went to church on Sunday morning; the women attended church more regularly than the men (See Table 1).

Although a few black Americans attend white chruches, Drake and Cayton[7] found that only 10 percent of Negro churchgoers in Chicago attended interracial churches and that, in the South, there is even less race mixing in the church. Atlanta is an example of a southern group that held membership mainly in black churches. However, they were not distributed evenly among the denominations; for example, three-fourths of the Golden Towers women were Protestant and belonged to several denominations (See Table 2). The majority were Baptist and Methodist and their spouses usually attended or held membership in their churches. Similarly, Brink and Harris[8] found that the Baptists continue to attract the largest number of Negroes accounting for 55 percent of church attendance, followed by the Methodist, who account for 18 percent of church attendance. About 10 percent of the Negro rank and file attend other Protestant denominations, 7 percent attend Fundamental and Catholic churches, respectively, while 3 percent expressed no religious preference.

The various denominational churches attended by blacks in Atlanta ranged from a small contemporary or traditional structures to large buildings with modern architecture. Those that draw disproportionally from well-to-do families do not necessarily have elaborate structures and facilities; some newer and more fully equipped churches have their basis of membership among people with moderate to low income.

Another comparison is the emotionalism manifested on Sunday morning. A few services were subdued while others were emotional. The extent of emotionalism, however, was inversely related to the socio-economic status of the membership; thus, the black churches in Atlanta were somewhat stratified. For example, the First Congregational church and the Friendship Baptist Church had the highest proportion of middle-class members while the Mount Zion Second Baptist Church membership was comprised of a sprinkling of middle-class and many working and low income members.

Table 1

Frequency of Church Attendance
by Husbands and Wives in
Golden Towers

Frequency	Number of	
	Hus-bands[a]	Wives[a]
Weekly	10	27
Bi-monthly	10	5
Monthly	6	4
Special occasions	1	1
None	1	- -
Total	28	37

[a]Number for which data on church attendance of husbands and wives were secured.

Table 2

Church Denominations of
Wives in Golden
Towers

Church denominations	Number of wives of each denomination[a]
Baptist	21
Methodist	8
Catholic	3
Congregational	2
Presbyterian	2
Episcopal	1
Lutheran	1
Total	38

[a]Number for which data on church affiliation of wives were secured.

The Mount Zion Second Baptist Church and the First Congregational Church were studied in detail because their geographical locations, furnishings, tone, process, and content of Sunday morning worship services were similar to other black churches in Atlanta. Besides, they contained in microcosm, the total range of Sunday morning worship experiences of Protestant residents in Atlanta.

Method.

The data for this study were obtained between September, 1969 and August, 1970. During the first two months, I attended several churches, including the Friendship Baptist, Wheat Street Baptist, and the Cosmopolitan African Methodist Episcopal churches. After selecting the First Congregational and Mount Zion Second Baptist churches for this study, during the next eight months, I attended each church every other Sunday morning, and engaged in participant observation. Following the service, I immediately wrote my field notes and studied the program; some quotations from the sermons and prayers were also written quickly in church. This was possible because, in one church, I often sat in the last pew while, in another church, tall people sometimes sat in front of me. Participant observation was supplemented with archival data, a tour of the churches, and intensive interviews with the minister, at each church, and the secretary at the First Congregational Church.

The Churches.

The First Congregational Church.

The First Congregational Church has provided its membership with varied experiences, including decision making. The establishment of the church represents one of its earliest decisions. Its origin goes back to shortly after the War Between the States when three Yale University graduates, including Edmund Asa Ware, established, under the auspices of the American Missionary Association, the Storrs School near the present location of the church. This was the first primary and elementary school for free men and their children in the city of Atlanta. After the New England missionaries had conducted religious services in the chapel of the Storrs School, the Congregational Church was organized May 26, 1867, with ten members, seven men and three women: from 1867 to 1894, the missionaries were pastors of the church.[9]

The members had also experienced selecting a site for their church.

It is located at the intersection of Houston and Courtland Streets in the eastern section of the Central Business District in close proximity to varied types of businesses, including nationally known hotels and the interstate highway system, that are seen from the church grounds (see Map of Atlanta, Chapter 1).

In 1908, the present structure was built on the original site, thereby, replacing the first small red brick church. The structure of the current church design is a more recent example of decision making. Its exterior is hybrid Spanish Mission architecture, which is unpretentious, yet distinctive and religious in design. The interior of the church consists of a high unobtrusive choir loft, located behind the pulpit and two balconies: one is on each side of the sanctuary, supported by columns. Moreover, the stained glass windows, two excepted, are reproductions of Biblical persons and saints, and they contribute to the traditional motif in the sanctuary.

The format of the Sunday morning service had four phases: The Call to Worship (music and prayer), The Message in Scripture and Song (scripture, prayer, and music), The Call to Prayer (prayer and music), and The Time of Sharing (prayer, music, offering, scripture, meditation, and preaching). Starting at 11 a.m., the service ended around 12:30 p.m. and represented another type of decision making in the church. The majority of the 75 to 100 members of the congregation were women, but young children and their parents sat together in silence.

A second function of the Sunday morning service at the First Congregational Church was to provide a chance for self-expression. It is conceptualized as overt participation in the service. By seating the congregation and passing the collection plates, the ushers, usually men, took an active part in the service. Nevertheless, only three people spoke during the service: the clerk read the church notices, the assistant pastor prayed the morning prayer, and the minister commented on the notices and delivered the sermon. What occurred was that the Sunday morning program provided only a few members with the opportunity to openly engage in the service, singing excepted.

On the other hand, Reverend McEwen, the pastor, expressed his ideas freely in his sermons, including the one entitled, "How Chirst Saves." He began by telling the congregation that many people were asking how they could be saved, especially young men and women who were taking narcotics. The pastor contended that the American culture was "becoming progressively anesthetic," which contributed to the hell that people were experiencing. Moreover, he continued, superficiality caused dissatisfaction: hence, some people attach a lot of significance to the name of their church and social club affiliations and the kinds of furs they wear. Since animals shed their fur in summer, the minister continued, with a sense of humor, "some of them have more sense than people." Another problem that he identified, in the society, is the youth cult or warmed over behavior "among black adults who attempt to look thirty or forty years younger than their age." He believed that the continuation of such practice will result in fewer marriages and children. The American society will then end up with a population like the one at the First Congregational Church: in his opinion, annual fertility rites will be needed to increase the population. The pastor informed the congregation that God saves from private and corporate hells and replaces them with a vigor of the spirit and a sense of security.

Following the service, the members of the congregation discussed the pastor's sermons. Some of them reacted adversely to the pastor's conservative views about the attire of adults and the youth cult, but there were others who considered his message timely. The minister's caution against putting too much emphasis on the name of one's church and social club membership received the same mixed reaction; nevertheless, the pastor, who had served his church thirty-eight years, was not afraid to speak out against what he called, "the Evils of the Society." During this sermon, as well as the remainder of them, the congregation sat in total silence and solemnity, but it was likely that its message and tone relieved tension, gave their spirit inspiration, and provided guidelines for daily living.

The third function of the First Congregational Church was to help the membership obtain prestige. However, there were only a few members, the pastor, clerk, ushers, and sometimes a soloist in the choir, who received prestige from participating on the Sunday morning church program. Since this group was constituted mainly of men, they received prestige more often than the women. On the other hand, the women obtained more prestige for their attire than the men. They attracted attention when they entered and left the church, stood for hymn singing, and talked outside the church. In considering the function of the church, it is possible that membership was a source of prestige for the whole congregation. Perhaps such prestige compensated for a relative lack of prestige in such settings as the workplace.

Mount Zion Second Baptist Church.

While collecting ethnographic data at the Mount Zion Second Baptist Church, I learned that this church also provided decision making opportunities for its membership. It made decisions regarding the organization of the church; for example, initially, a group decided to establish it by separating amicably and Christlike from the Friendship Baptist Church.[10] The next major decision was made in 1868, when the members decided to worship in an edifice located at Piedmont and Baker Streets in northeast Atlanta (see Map of Atlanta, Chapter 1). Between 1880 and 1926, two fires destroyed the church, and two ministers resigned; each of them organized a separate Baptist church, but the membership remained at the original church until 1956. In that year, Atlanta acquired the land to construct an expressway. As a result, the church decided to locate on Boulevard and Irwin Streets in Northeast Atlanta, a short distance from the Central Business District (see Map of Atlanta, Chapter 1).

They had also selected a church design. The structure is contemporary architecture, and the sanctuary has a beige color scheme and a high ceiling with exposed beams and recess lighting.

The time of the Sunday Morning Church service was another decision that was made by the Mount Zion Second Baptist Church. It was determined that it would begin at 10:45 a.m. and end at 1:00 p.m. The seating arrangement, during the Sunday morning service, was still another major decision made by the church. It was based on role in the service and age and sex of worshipers. Approximatley 75 to 85 percent of the 275 to 300 member congregation, on Sunday morning, was female. Of this number, twenty-five to fifty worshipers were children. The order of the service was still another decision that the church made. It was comprised of The Call to Worship (meditation, prayer, music, and scripture), A Time of Sharing (offering, prayer, announcements, music, recognition and welcome to guest), and the Sermon.

What I found was that the decisions made at the Mount Zion Second Baptist Church reflected age, sex, and role grading, more so, than the decisions that were made at the First Congregational Church. This finding indicates that this Baptist Church was probably stricter than the First Congregational Church. If, indeed, this were the case, there were probably multiple reasons, such as a wider gap in the socioeconomic status of the baptist congregation, along with a less educated membership, than is found at the congregational church. If these circumstances hold, in all likelihood, detailed decision making on Sunday morning was advantageous.

The Sunday morning worship program, including the offertory, gave. the pastor and his congregation another outlet, an opportunity for self-expression. Just before the offering was taken, four to five men stood behind three or more tables, located in front of the altar, and appealed to the congregation for a good collection. After the offertory prayer, they received and counted it. But it was the minister who gave the offertory prayer. He emphasized generous support of the church by praying, "May our giving be symbolic of our personal dedication to Thee; Help us to do Thy will;" besides, the prayer seemed to equate one's personal dedication to God and His will with the extent of financial support to the church.

The ushers were the next members to express themselves. They directed the congregation to the offering tables by sending them, in ritualized order, determined by the seating pattern, and returning them to their seat, down the opposite aisle, the A-men corners (rows of seats to the left and right of the pulpit), excepted. At this time, the entire congregation participated in the service: they stood, lined up, and took their offering to the tables. The music helped transform this part of the service into a religious holiday and reinforce the theme of generous giving. It was accomplished through rhythmic songs, including "Count Your Blessings" and "See What God Has Done For You", along with slow common meter hymns, such as "Amazing Grace," which consists of "I'm not worried 'bout my soul, 'cause I fixed it with Jesus a long time ago." They seemed to cause a sense of emotional, mental, and physical ecstasy and freedom, that reduced tension and helped the congregation contribute liberally to the offering. Hence, the strong once a week financial program, at the Mount Zion Second Baptist Church, included speeches, prayer, music, marching, and contributions, supported by its pastor, The Rev. E. R. Searcy.

That the sermon provided additional opportunities for self-expression was also evident. Thus, the pastor covered a variety of subjects, in each sermon, including selection of marital partners, prejudice among blacks, faith in God, spiritual power, through Christian living, healing power, and deliverance. On a particular Sunday, for example, he spoke on the subject, "New Power in Human Life." The pastor told the congregation that, by imitating whites, blacks are trying to receive new power; for example, he noted that black families had learned from white families to place emphasis on family connections, family blood, family dignity, and marrying their daughters to the "right" young men. He illustrated this observation be relating a story about a black female celebrity. When he was growing up, there were only three cities in the United States that had a Negro society: Washington, D.C.; Atlanta, and Thomasville, Georgia. A prominent woman, one of his school mates, lived in one of them; each time that a young man asked her to marry him, her family and friends told her that he was too black, too ugly, or too poor. When he recently saw the woman, her hair was white, and she was still unmarried; but he knew some unattractive girls who were married to fine young black men. What he advised the young women to do, was to ask God to give them a husband.

Then the minister illustrated the source of new power in human life by relating the story of the leper who told Jesus, "If Thou wilt, thou canst make me clean, and Jesus answered, I choose to do so -- Be thou clean. Then Jesus touched the leper and he was made clean." This spiritual power, the minister continued, helped the leper to see better, to think better, and to eat and sleep in his own home. He then inspired the congregation by telling them that God is still able and willing to put new power in one who pursues his life's work. Moreover, he encouraged the congregation to use their direct line to God, if their mind and spirit were torn up or burdened down, if their medication had failed them, if they felt comfortless. While this and other sermons were being preached, the members of the congregation clapped their hands, rocked their bodies forward and backward and side to side, said A-Men, patted their feet, cried, and shouted. In fact, there were only a few adults who sat quietly while the pastor delivered an eloquent, but passionate sermon.

A Discussion of the Two Churches.

The First Congregational Church and the Mount Zion Second Baptist Church were similar religious institutions in the Atlanta black sub-society. Thus, it was not surprising that they were organized only a year apart, and, though the architecture varies, that each had constructed at least two church buildings. It follows that the message in both churches centered around hope and deliverance, but the style of dissemination was teaching in the Congregational church while preaching was usually employed in the Baptist church. More-over, the men in both churches held the most prestigious positions, but this was more characteristic of the Congregational church than of the Baptist church. In fact, with only the minister's permission, a male member of the Congregational church, periodically, redecorat-ed the sanctuary. The women appeared satisfied with male dominance, a probable consequence of their satisfaction with prestige from church membership, the success of their husbands, and, in some cases, their own success. A majority of the women worked in the business sector, the public school system, and the local colleges. Another reason that probably helps explain the women's acceptance of their relatively unimportant role in the church is that they belonged to numerous social clubs and obtained recognition through elaborate entertainment.

On the other hand, the women in the Mount Zion Second Baptist Church read the notices, constituted the majority of the ushers and the choir, assisted with communion, and kept the service lively. This type of participation was essential, for many of them were domestics or worked on other low paying jobs; besides a lack of prestigious and authority bearing jobs, as well as husbands, in some cases, left a gap in the women's lives, which was somewhat filled by emotionalism. Hence, for many blacks in this church, overt participation assisted in their adaptation to external circumstances.

The two churches differed in several other ways, including the length of the Sunday morning service. The Baptists spent more time at church than the Congregationalists and there was more segregation in the seating pattern, based on age, sex, and role in service, at the Baptist church than at the Congregational church. A probable explanation for the relative long service at the Baptist church was that sometimes business matters were reported, during the service, that were usually discussed in church meetings at the Congregational church. What this means is that Sunday morning was about the only time that the Baptist minister could discuss business matters for a somewhat large number of members. Judging by this pattern, and from what I observed in the churches, it is safe to conclude that there was more formality in the Congregational church service than in the Sunday morning service at the Baptist church.

Another point of comparison between the two churches was the attitude of the membership toward their pastor. Although both ministers were highly respected, the Baptist congregation, unlike the Congregational members, seemed to revere their pastor. Moreover, the relationship between the Baptist minister and his members provided still another avenue, especially for the women, to express themselves. This was demonstrated through conversation and attention from the minister and gift giving; some women, for example, took home cooked meals to him in his church office. The financial patterns of the churches were also different; the Baptists appeared to contribute as much money to the church as their circumstances permitted while this was not the case in the Congregational church.

Nevertheless, the two churches were more similar than different. The worshipers in both churches, as well as those in other churches, in the Atlanta black subsociety, believed that the Sunday morning church service rounded out their lives and gave them inspiration to carry on their daily routine, a conclusion supported by Brink and Harris,[11] who found that 76 percent of the blacks interviewed in their national survey believe that the church is a helpful influence in the life of Negro people.

Social Organizations.

Since slavery, the church has continued as the major voluntary association. However, a larger variety of social organizations, on the local, regional, and national levels, including men's groups, have been developed.

A number of the men's organizations in the Atlanta black subsociety provided varied opportunities for decision making as well as for self-expression, and prestige. They included the Superb Viceroy, which gave mixed cocktail and stag parties, picnics, and an annual husband and wife out of town weekend trip; and the Torchbearers, who socialized at their meetings and raised scholarship money. Moreover, a few of the men belonged to the Guardsmen, a national social and civic organization, nationally organized fraternities, the Professional Hunting and Fishing Club, local male and mixed bridge clubs, and the National and American Bridge Associations. As these examples demonstrate, the men decided social and charitable events, a source of some prestige, and expressed themselves by demonstrating their skills in catching animals and sea life and playing bridge.

Similar to the men, the Atlanta women participated in different types of organizations that provided decision making, self-expression, and prestige opportunities. An unusual group was the "Greensboro" Social Club, that consisted of Atlanta residents who migrated from "Greensboro," Georgia. It met the fourth Sunday in each month, for approximately two hours, to conduct devotions, hear a brief speech on a modern American problem, plan their future activities, including a fund raising campaign for cancer research, and socialize. Following the business meetings, in the summer, the members ate ice cream and cookies and, in the winter, they ate sandwiches and drank ice tea while sharing hometown news. The club continued in Atlanta the congenial relations that they experienced in Greensboro, as well as maintained an emotional link with their friends and kinsmen in Greensboro.

Among middle class black women, in Atlanta, bridge clubs were the usual female organizations. They were called varied names, such as Casual Cliques, Circlettes, Chums, Dina's Gorenettes, Hearts, Jasmine, Jovial Coterie, Juts, Just Us, Lazy Me's, Nancy, the Relaxers, and the VIPs.

On a typical bridge occasion, the hostess greeted the guests and directed them to the den or family room for a cocktail hour. The women expressed themselves by talking about cooking, new grandchildren, difficult names that black parents give their children to enhance their self-concept, clothing, jewelry, and furniture. The cocktail hour was followed by a brief business session in which plans were made for other social events and a buffet meal. While the guests were serving their plates and eating, they complimented the hostess on the attractive and delicious food, a source of much prestige and pleasure. After dinner, the women played several rounds of bridge while they continued conversation and laughter. The final phase of the meeting centered around tallying the scores and awarding prizes, such as evening bags, leather pocketbooks, electric food warmers, jewelry, and spice racks, and complimenting the hostess on her gift selections.

Social organizations were a major source of power, self-expression, and prestige, in the black subsociety, in Atlanta. It was possible that the large number of same sex groups further enhanced such opportunities, especially among women.

Coordinating Council of Northwest Clubs.

This civic organization also gave its members several opportunities to participate in decision making. The initial decision centered around organizing the Coordinating Council of Northwest Clubs. It was made by B. F. Bullock, and a few other residents in Collier Heights, who called a joint meeting of the two or three organized neighborhood clubs in this area. Of course, since that time, the number of organized clubs, in the Council, has grown to thirty-five and membership continued to be available to all organized clubs in the area.

Another early decision made by the Council concerned their meeting time. They decided to meet bimonthly and usually met on schedule. However, they had started meeting only when a crisis arose and there were only three meetings between September, 1969 and August 1, 1970.

Since the Council focused on leading protest against efforts to rezone residential property for commercial and apartment uses in Collier Heights, there were many opportunities for self-expression. However, one group, called the Watch Dog Committee, probably had a greater opportunity for self-expression than other members, because it was their duty to spearhead protests. To their surprise, it was not long before one of their members turned on them and became known as a "White Dog." The work of the Watch Dog Committee included informing the Coordinating Council of all attempts to rezone the area. This was accomplished by assigning a member of the Committee the responsibility of riding around and looking in all trees, along the streets in Collier Heights, to locate rezoning notices. Because white business interests, the Council said, were powerful and sometimes influenced the zoning committee to post the rezoning notices among the branches, this was a difficult task. When this occurred, sometimes business interests got areas rezoned before the notices were located; subsequently, blacks attempted, unsuccessfully, to get the order reversed.

By holding and participating in meetings when rezoning notices were found, prior to a hearing, the Council engaged in decision making and obtained an opportunity to express themselves. After unity was achieved, which was not always easy, at least one spokesman was chosen to represent Collier Heights at the hearings; besides, all the Collier Heights residents were requested to attend them. Sometimes several bus loads of the residents appeared at the zoning sessions, which they believed made a favorable impression on the Atlanta Zoning Committee.

The estimation of the effect of their spokesman and group attendance, at the hearings, was accurate, for the city officials soon decided that the Collier Heights Community should make a study of the types of buildings and their locations that could be constructed in the area. Subsequently, an expert planner was hired, by the Coordinating Council, to plan the area. As a result of this plan, the cases that reached the Atlanta Zoning Committee, which conflicted with its stipulations, were sometimes defeated. However, in spite of the efforts, time, and money invested, the area was still characterized

51

by a number of commercial businesses, but not nearly so many as there would have been without the Council.

When the Council won a case, there was much group prestige. Like membership in the Congregational Church, membership in the Council, at such times, brought group prestige and, of course, the leaders received some personal prestige for directing the protest.

Conclusions.

The aim in this chapter was to compare the functions of the First Congregational Church, the Mount Zion Second Baptist Church, several social organizations, and the Coordinating Council of Northwest Clubs, in the Atlanta black subsociety, and relate them to the adaptation of blacks in the society. It was found that the organizations shared a number of functions, including decision making. The religious associations provided an opportunity for Atlanta residents to make decisions concerning church location and construction, the Sunday morning program format, content, and length, and time of implementation, seating arrangement, and participation on the program. On the other hand, the social organizations gave members the opportunity to decide the activities of the groups, frequency, format, and content of meetings, menus, and prizes while the Council provided decision making opportunities regarding its formation, meeting schedule, and zoning attempts.

The religious and social organizations and Council also provided opportunities for self-expression. In the churches, ideas concerning social and religious issues and the pastor's conservative views, about such topics were expressed. It was also found that both churches provided an opportunity for participation in the services, including seating the congregation, singing, and carrying out tasks, such as reading announcements, praying, collecting the offering, and directing the congregation to the offering tables. On the other hand, family, household, social, and hometown news were talked about at social club meetings; besides, they gave the black residents, in Atlanta, an opportunity to demonstrate their hunting, fishing, socializing, card playing, culinary, and gift selection skills. The primary source of expression, in the Council, was the opportunity to search for commercial zoning notices and decide and implement strategies to defeat such zoning attempts.

Another function of the organizations was to award prestige to their members. In the religious groups, it was derived from church membership, participation on the Sunday morning program or in the service, and wearing attractive clothing. Of course, social club affiliation enabled members to obtain prestige from well planned and implemented meetings and programs, excellent choice and quality of gifts, and contributions to worthy projects; and, when the Council succeeded in preventing residential areas from being rezoned, the members received prestige.

Another conclusion is that the functions of religious, social, and civic organizations assisted blacks in adapting to society. Since they did not hold a large number of prestigious and authority bearing positions,[12] they received only relatively few chances to make decisions, express themselves, and receive prestige on their jobs. Consequently, by providing these opportunities, the religious, social, and civic organizations functioned to fill a gap in the lives of their membership. Moreover, the message in the sermons and the conversation, during the social occasions and activities of the Coordinating Council of Northwest clubs, also functioned as an adaptive mechanism. They provided release from tension, enhancement of self-importance, and rounded out the lives of black Atlantans.

As a result of not receiving invitations to join particular voluntary associations and the lack of appropriate space and money to participate, the lower and working classes were virtually excluded from membership in social organizations. Thus, all blacks in Atlanta did not have equal access to the adaptive functions of social groups, which may somewhat explain why the working and lower classes made more use of the church. Moreover, although all blacks in the Atlanta black subsociety can benefit from the functions of religious, social, and civic organizations, the lower the social class, the greater the need for sources of adaptation in society. Nevertheless, the Atlanta Chapter of Jack and Jill is a vivid illustration of a voluntary association that had long helped black middle class families, as well as other families, in Atlanta, and throughout America, adapt to society.

NOTES

1. R. M. MacIver. THE SOCIETY. Chicago: University of Chicago Press, 1970, pp. 12-15.

2. Melvin Tumin. SOCIAL STRATIFICATION. Englewood Cliffs: Prentice Hall, Inc., 1969.

3. W. E. B. Dubois. SOME EFFECTS OF AMERICAN NEGROES FOR THEIR BETTERMENT. Atlanta: Atlanta University Press, 1898, p. 6.

4. E. Franklin Frazier. THE NEGRO CHURCH IN AMERICA. New York: Schecker Books, 1963, p. 14.

5. Jack C. Ross and Raymond H. Wheeler. BLACK BELONGING. Westport: Greenwood Press, 1971, p. 203.

6. William Brink and Louis Harris. THE NEGRO REVOLUTION. New York: Simon and Schuster, 1964, pp. 220-221.

7. St. Clair Drake and Horace R. Cayton. BLACK METROPOLIS, Vol. II. New York: Harper and Row Publishers, 1945, p. 413.

8. William Brink and Louis Harris. THE NEGRO REVOLUTION op. cit., pp. 220-221.

9. The First Congregational Church. 100 YEARS FOR CHRIST, 1867-1967. Atlanta: First Congregational Church, 1967, p. 8.

10. Mount Zion Second Baptist Church. CENTENNIAL BOOKLET, 1868-1968. Atlanta: Mount Zion Second Baptist Church, 1968, p. 1.

11. William Brink and Louis Harris. THE NEGRO REVOLUTION. op. city., pp. 220-221.

12. U. S. Department of Labor. THE ATLANTA URBAN EMPLOY-MENT SURVEY, July, 1968 - June, 1967. Atlanta: Bureau of Labor Statistics, 1969, pp. 7-8.

CHAPTER FIVE

THE NEIGHBORHOOD

The Atlanta black middle class also occupies a number of neighborhoods, including Golden Towers, in the black subsociety. Because the location, origin, and interaction that go on in neighborhoods was the essence of behavior, these topics are the focus of this chapter.

On July 13, 1955, the founder-developer purchased Golden Towers, which is located on forty acres of land in Collier Heights. Some three years later, settlement began with the home of the founder-developer, located almost at the South end of Woodmere Drive, and another family settled, in that year, in the northern section of the same street (see Figure 1, Chapter 6). Golden Towers was a dense wooded area, and the mail was delivered to the residents in mailboxes located on Bankhead Highway (see Figure 1, Chapter 1). Sometime around February or March, 1959, the residents received a notice to move their mailboxes to the front of their homes; by March 15 of that year, home mail delivery had begun.

Origin of the Golden Towers Residents.

Because the Census data show that blacks in Atlanta have more often migrated from other parts of Georgia than from outside the state, I decided to find out whether Golden Towers residents are similar to the remainder of blacks in Atlanta. As indicated in Table 1, 48.1 percent of the males and 34 percent of the females in Golden Towers were natives of Atlanta; and 48 percent of the population had lived in this city less than a year to more than forty years. These data suggest that a majority of the residents were migrants to Atlanta, who comprised part of the sizeable in migration movement to this city in recent decades. Of this group, only five males and six females came from other states and, with one male exception, this group came from other southern states. Thus, in respect to place of origin, the Golden Towers residents were typical of the black population in Atlanta.

Table 1

Native Born Population and Number of Years
In-Migrants in Golden Towers Have Lived
in the City of Atlanta

Native born and number of years spent in Atlanta	Total number[a]	Percent	Male number[a]	Percent	Female number[a]	Percent
Natives	30	41	17	48	13	34
0-5 years	2	3	1	3	1	3
6-10 years	2	3	1	3	1	3
11-15 years	5	7	2	6	3	8
16-25 years	9	12	1	3	8	21
26-40 years	21	29	13	37	8	21
41 years and over	4	5	0	0	4	10
Total	73	100	35	100	38	100

[a]Number of cases for whom native born and migrant data were secured.

Why Did the Golden Towers Residents Migrate to Atlanta?

Since a sizeable number of the Golden Towers residents migrated from outside Atlanta, the respondents were asked why they settled in this city. They reported that the men migrated to Atlanta to seek better employment, obtain a college education, better educational opportunities for their children, experience better living conditions, and move with their spouses or relatives. Though varied causes were given for men's migration to Atlanta, better employment and educational opportunities were the most frequently mentioned reasons, in that order, for male migration. The women came to Atlanta for similar reasons, such as to accompany the head of the family, join the head of the family who was either a native Atlantan, or who had gone to Atlanta and determined that the entire family should live in this city, job transfer, or to accompany their parents. On the other hand, the reasons given most often for women's migration to Atlanta were to accompany the head of household and attend college; thus, the men and women migrated to Atlanta mainly to obtain a college education.

The remainder of this chapter describes the social behavior among the residents in Golden Towers to determine whether social contacts exist among people, from varied parts of Georgia and Atlanta, that tie them together in neighborly relations. The type of social behavior used to answer this question were neighborhood club participation, telephoning, visiting, helping patterns, and parties. Since the neighborhood club was the largest geographical group that attempted to promote a spirit of togetherness, it will now be discussed.

The Neighborhood Club.

Similar to the churches, bridge clubs, and Jack and Jill, in the larger black subsociety, the neighborhood club is a voluntary association. It was organized by the wife of the founder-developer of Golden Towers during the fall of 1958 to promote a spirit of togetherness and to aid neighbors to work, as a group, to eliminate problems relating to the upkeep of the neighborhood. During the early years of settlement, neighbors were friendly, and the men and women worked together in this organization to resolve such problems as sewerage disposal, water supply, and commercial rezoning. As soon as these problems were solved, the men withdrew from the club, but some of the women continued to meet. Several days before each meeting, the women received a notice or telephone call reminding them to attend.

The women met four times (March, April, May, June) between September, 1969 and June, 1970. During the March meeting, new officers were elected and installed, the $1.00 monthly membership fee was determined, and the second Friday in each month, the summer excepted, was chosen as the meeting date. They also decided that the meeting place would be designated by the alphabetical listing of the membership and, at the conclusion of the meeting, refreshments were served. During the remainder of the meetings, there was far less business; for example, in the April meeting, the main issue was the census type questionnaire that I mailed to all residents, requesting socioeconomic data and, during the May meeting, tribute was paid to the neighborhood mothers and one mother was awarded a plaque. After a brief meeting in June, the women and their husbands shared a covered dish supper in celebration of all neighborhood fathers. Though only one mother received a plaque, during the Mother's Day celebration, and the women gave it to her, a supper was given by all the women to celebrate Father's Day.

There were other activities, courtesies, and parties that were sponsored by the neighborhood club. The club members also collected funds from the entire neighborhood for use during bereavement and sickness. However, the women noted that one's socioeconomic status or relationship to the more prestigious neighbors determined the extent or even whether neighborhood courtesies were received. Hence, when some families experienced bereavement, the women hosted a meal in the home of the bereaved and sent flowers. When there was an illness in those same homes, they sent flowers and cards. Of course, other families, on such occasions, received only some or none of these courtesies. What concerned some of the women was that neighborhood courtesies, begun to unite the group, had an isolating effect.

Besides these activities, the neighborhood club sponsored a Christmas party in the basement of a neighbor's home. The members and their spouses sang, danced, and ate. The attendance at the Christmas party as well as at the neighborhood club meetings was low. The unequal socioeconomic status of neighbors and conflicting Yuletide activities, the women said, accounted for limited participation in the Christmas party. On the other hand, because emphasis was placed on social matters rather than on upkeep of the neighborhood, some residents did not attend the neighborhood club meetings while other neighbors did not attend because they found it difficult to interact with some of the women. As far as I could determine, the latter situation arose because the neighborhood was a heterogeneous group. With a more uniform socioeconomic group, it is likely that the activities would not exist at all, or that there would have been better participation.

Telephoning.

After I learned that the intensity of social behavior on the neighborhood level was low, I next studied interpersonal behavior. The data indicate that interaction between households in Golden Towers was female dominated and dyadic. This type of social behavior means that each woman had only one close associate in the neighborhood, or that she had more than one person with whom she was friendly, but she usually associated with each woman separately. The dyadic relations were most vivid in telephone behavior, house visitations, and helping patterns, but less vivid in party patterns.

Telephoning was the most frequent type of contact between Golden Towers neighbors. To understand the social function of telephoning, business calls were excluded. As shown in Table 2, the women in

Golden Towers telephoned each other more than men telephoned each other; besides, there was little telephoning between the sexes. However, upon further inquiry, I found that the women called members of their extended group or friends who lived in other sections of Atlanta.

Visiting.

The visiting patterns in Golden Towers were very similar to the telephoning behavior. As noted in Table 3, though women visited each other more than men visited their friends, visiting among neighbors was infrequent. What else is interesting is that some men, as well as women, had several contacts while others either did not visit in Golden Towers, or only occasionally. Nevertheless, the men and women in this neighborhood desired to visit people, which was satisfied, like telephoning, by visiting their kinsmen and friends in other sections of Atlanta. Of course, another way both sexes satisfied this need was by participating in voluntary associations in the black subsociety, as discussed in Chapter 4, and by developing friendships in their places of employment.

I also desired to know who the women were who visited their neighbors. The data indicate that the older the women were, the more likely they were to visit frequently, a probable consequence of greater economic and emotional security among older than younger women. What I am suggesting is that economic security may contribute to development of a confident and outgoing personality. On the other hand, the women who did not visit their neighbors included those with an educational level ranging from ninth grade to extensive college experience, housewives and white collar workers, and an even mumber of migrants and natives. In general, however, those women who visited six or more neighbors were more often between forty and forty-nine years of age, migrant, college educated, and blue collar and white collar workers.

Helping Patterns.

It appears that neighbors preferred assisting each other, especially men, than socializing together. The husbands and wives gave varied assistance to each other; for example, men skilled in particular household repair jobs, upon request, gave advice to their neighbors. Then, there were men with varied skills who worked for their female neighbors. In one case, a husband who worked part time as an interior decorator, in addition to his regular job, had made draperies for

Table 2

Telephoning Patterns among
Residents in Golden
Towers

Number of residents[a]	Number of neighbors telephoned
Men	
1	3
1	5
1	6
2	2
4	1
9[b]	
Women	
3	4
4	0
4	5
6	6 and over
7	1
8	3
9	2
41[b]	

[a]Number of cases for which data on telephoning patterns were secured.

[b]Total.

Table 3

Home Visitation Patterns among
Residents in Golden
Towers

Number of residents[a]	Number of neighbors visited
Men	
2	2
3	3
3	6 and over
8	1
23	0
39[b]	
Women	
2	5
5	2
5	3
6	0
7	4
7	6 and over
9	1
41[b]	

[a]Number of cases for which data on visitation patterns were secured.

[b]Total.

62

a number of the women while another husband, who was a music teacher, had taught piano lessons to a neighbor's children. There was another helping pattern centered around parties. Some men and women gave invitations to their neighbors to attend their social club affairs, even though the invitations were not always reciprocated. According to the respondents, the neighbors were people whom the host and hostess desired at their social event and was not related to the day tc day or even month to month interaction between the couples. There was, however, another helping pattern, especially among the women. They helped each other by serving as hostess or guests at bridge parties when a member or another guest unexpectedly could not attend. Because the women did not like to play bridge at their own club meetings, for it prevented them from carrying out their duties, in certain prescribed ways, they were extremely delighted when a neighbor helped them by accepting an invitation at the last minute to come to their bridge meeting.

Parties.

Though not as frequent as helping behavior, some couples in Golden Towers invited their neighbors, as well as other people, to their parties. In fact, twenty-two of the forty-one households included neighbors among their party guests. the majority of the residents in Golden Towers who attended parties in their neighborhood received such privilege about once a year, because the residents did not often give house parties. As noted in Chapter 4, a majority of their party behavior was sponsored by social organizations. Nevertheless, the women invited up to two couples from their neighborhood to the parties that they gave in their homes; and such couples usually lived on the same street or in the same section as the host and hostess. Thus, mixed parties were also infrequent behavior among some neighbors in Golden Towers. Another type of group activity was bridge meetings; although only one hostess sponsored each bridge session, it was within the context of a group. Because of the nine or more members in each bridge club, each entertained once every nine months or even less often. It was thus concluded that parties were not a major source of contact among Golden Towers as neighbors.

Neighborly Behavior.

Although social behavior inside the home has been discussed, it should be stated that there were ephemeral contacts between residents on their lawns, doorsteps, and patios. Nevertheless, neighborly interaction was localized in dyadic relations, parties excepted. Such dyadic behavior was usually between female neighbors, who lived next door to each other, across the street from each other, on the same street, or in the same general area of the neighborhood. Besides, the greatest number of social contacts were localized in the southern part of the neighborhood, where houses and annual income were more sufficient.

Summary.

As shown in Figure 1, the residents in Golden Towers had an incipient interaction system comprised of participation in a neighborhood club, telephoning, visiting, helping patterns, parties, and ephemeral contact. As also indicated in Figure 1, 5 percent of the residents did not have either party, telephone, or visiting contact with their neighbors. Then, of course, the same percentage either had only telephone contact with their neighbors or had telephone and party contact with them. Hence, almost 15 percent of the residents were on the periphery of the already incipient neighborhood system. On the other hand, a much larger percentage of the neighbors either visited and telephoned or attended parties, visited and telephoned at least one neighbor. In summary, the graphic description of social behavior in Golden Towers illustrates that there were levels of contact starting with none on the first level, only telephone contact on the second level, party and telephone contact on the third level, visiting and telephone contact on the fourth level, and party attendance, visiting, and telephone contact on the fifth level. Moreover, Figure 1 indicates that less than half of the residents were at the center of the incipient interaction system.

The description of Golden Towers suggests that dyads, parties, and the neighborhood club were loci of neighborhood behavior. This social contact helped satisfy certain needs as to communicate, but it did not add up to a community type situation. Neighborly relations, among residents from different parts of Georgia, did not tie them together in a strong emotional bond or give them a sense of belonging to the neighborhood as a totality. The area, therefore, is a neighborhood, but not a community in which meaningful relations outside the home exist.

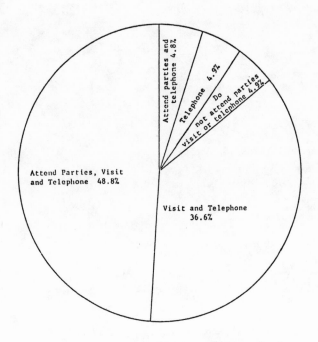

Figure 1. Interpersonal Relations in Golden Towers

§§§§§

NOTES

1. City of Atlanta. LAND LOT BOOK, 230, 249, 259. Atlanta: City of Atlanta

CHAPTER SIX

THE HOME AND ITS ENVIRONS

Even though there is incipient interaction on the neighborhood level, a great deal of emphasis is placed on the home setting. Nevertheless, there is only a small empirical literature on the physical setting of the household. Because understanding the home environment provides a broader perspective on family behavior, as much as describing the home and its environs, this essay concentrates on the functions of the Golden Towers home. Mead[1] related that the middle class home functions as "a sort of stage set" where family members enact their roles. The furniture for such settings is either new or refurbished and rearranged with care. Mead[2] also observed that in the middle class family, "Each child is given its property; a room to itself is the ideal, the toys and books and tools are personal possessions, respect for which is enforced among brothers and sisters. Hence, Mead takes a symbolic-use approach to the home setting. After doing a household inventory in Liverpool, of "All items of furniture in the living room, dining room, parlour, sitting room, morning room, study, and other living rooms, and the principal furnishings of the kitchen," Chapman[3] also described the household from a use perspective: it is thus a setting for "behavior directed toward fulfillment of certain discernible ends, nutrition, shelter, education, and the like." Instead of the use function, Goffman[4] states that the equipment in a home setting has a symbolic function; It "is evidence of conformity to certain life standards of taste appropriate to a status group or evidence of wealth," a view that supports Mead's implicit symbolic function of the setting in the middle class household.

After reading these reports, I began searching for similar studies about the homes of black families. Unable to find them, I used the symbolic-use perspective of the household setting as suggested by Mead, Goffman, and Chapman. Also, Chapman's inventory method was used as a guide for this essay.

Method.

The inventory method was used to obtain data about the interior and exterior of the homes in Golden Towers. This method is conceptualized in this study as a data gathering technique that itemizes, describes, and categorizes the interior and exterior of the homes and their furnishings, by doing inventories and taking notes and pictures. The photography component included taking pictures of the interior and exterior of homes. To photograph the exterior of the homes, I asked each female spouse for such permission. While taking the pictures, I took notes on their styles; subsequently, I drew a diagram of the neighborhood with the location of the homes and a legend identifying the styles of the homes (see Figure 1, Chapter 6). On the other hand, after doing each household inventory, I sometimes asked the respondent for permission to take pictures of the interior of her home.

During the household inventories, I asked the residents census type questions. The initial inquiries were: How many rooms and full and half baths are there in your home? What are the names and uses of each room? Once these data were collected, I asked the respondent to allow me to identify and itemize the furnishings and window dressings by room. Because this request made the residents suspicious of my purpose in their neighborhood, this was often a difficult task. The two questions that suggested their suspicion were: Are you an agent of the white man? Have you been sent here by the Internal Revenue Department? I assured each inquisitor that I was only a wife, mother, and a student. This simple explanation gave me the freedom to conduct the inventory in thirty-one of the thirty-nine homes that participated in the Golden Towers study. Of course, a number of women reluctantly let me see their master bedroom, and two other women did not let me see it. In still another home, I was given full access to the downstairs areas, which were devoted to eating, relaxing, and entertaining, but I was denied access to the upstairs living quarters that had "the look of 'story book beautiful,'" the neighbors say. Here, again, I sensed that the bedroom area was not only private for the spouses, but also for the whole family. Nevertheless, the relative importance of the master bedroom was seen in its careful and elaborate decoration.

Before conducting the furnishing inventory, I received preparation for it in a well known department store in Atlanta. A man and woman, at different times in its Home Advisory Department, taught me how to recognize furniture styles, and gave me a working definition

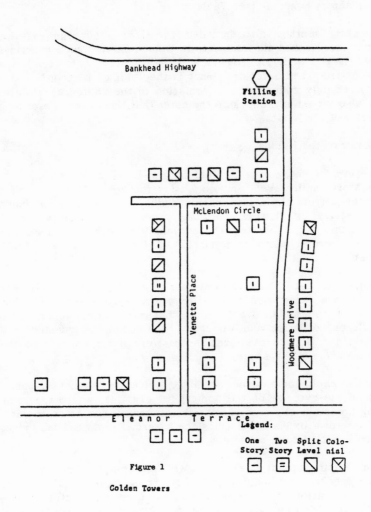

Figure 1

Colden Towers

69

of traditional, contemporary, and eclectic rooms. While receiving these instructions and reading Chapman's book, I constructed a Furnishing Inventory Schedule (see Table 1).

The inventory method also included questions about the exterior of the homes. I asked the residents in Golden Towers such questions as: What is the style of your home? What kind of material was used to construct the exterior? What is the color of its trim? These questions not only added some information to the photographic data, but they also served as a check on the notes that I had taken describing the exterior of the homes.

The Exterior of the Homes.

The exteriors of the homes in Golden Towers, as seen in Figure 1, are one story, split level, and colonial structures. They set back some distance from the street, surrounded by manicured lawns made more attractive by flowers, shrubbery, and trees. The width of the lots ranges from 100 to 445 feet and the depth is 150 to 358 feet. The average width is some 121.06 feet, the average depth is 182 feet.

After collecting data about the environs of the home, the next task was to obtain a description of their exterior. What I found was that thirty-one of the homes were brick, four were brick veneer, two were built out of brick and wood, and one had a brick veneer and panel exterior. Due to oversight, notes were not recorded for the thirty-ninth home in this study.

The roof of each home blends with the brick, brick veneer, panel, or wood on the exterior of the homes; for example, where the brick and trim are pink, the roof is pinkish; or, where the brick is dark, the roof is brown or black. Besides the exterior, roofs and mailboxes blend into a unified color scheme.

The home environs and exteriors in Golden Towers are seen in a one story ranch, the typical neighborhood house, which with greater or lesser elaboration could be any one of the other single story dwellings. This reddish roof house sits on a 110 feet wide and 150 feet deep lot. It is constructed of red brick with white decorative lattices at its windows; the trim on the windows, doors, the eagle shaped design on the wrought iron door, and the double garage doors are white. A cement drive extends from the garage to the street, and a cement walkway extends from the front door to the street. There

TABLE 1
Home Furnishing Inventory Schedule
(Use One Sheet Per Room)

Name of Room	Name of Each Piece of Furniture in Room	Purpose of Each Piece of Furniture	Color Scheme

(Use back of sheet if addition space is needed)

Draperies (Color, length, fabric)_____
Carpet (Color, partial or complete floor covering)_____
Type of Furniture that Dominates Room_____
Type of Paintings (Original, copies)_____
Use of Wall Mirrors (Number, Location, size)_____
Miscellaneous_____

TABLE 2

Assessed Tax Value and Probable Market Value of Golden Towers Dwellings

Assessed tax value categories (&)	Probable market value based on assessed tax value (&)	Total number of dwellings in tax category	Percent of dwellings in assessed tax category
7280	18,200-24,200	10	24.4
10,340-12,780	25,850-31,950	18	43.9
13,060-17,340	32,650-43,350	10	24.4
23,810-27,650	59,525-69,125	2	4.9
Church parsonage tax exempt		1	2.4
Total		41	100.0

Forty perrcent of market value.
Number of cases for which data on assessed tax value of dwellings in Golden Towers were secured.

are two lamp posts, one on either side of the cement walk on the rich green lawn; a large cedar tree sits to the right front of the home near a large pine tree that sits nearer the street. The assessed value of this home in 1970 was $13,180 and its probable market value was approximately $33,000. As seen in Table 2, the probable market value of the Golden Towers homes in that year ranged from $18,200 to $69,125.

The Interior of the Homes.

The ethnographic data about the physical setting of the homes were even more varied than the findings about the exteriors of the homes and their environs. For example, as the lot sizes suggest, the number of rooms in each home varied. Excluding car porches, garages, foyers, furnace rooms, patios, sun parlors, halls, and trophy alcoves, but including the basement rooms that had been completed and furnished, the number of rooms in each home ranged from seven to fifteen; more than one half of the Golden Towers families lived in homes with ten to fifteen rooms, and the most typical home had ten or eleven rooms (see Table 3).

TABLE 3

Size of Homes in Golden Towers

Number of Rooms	Number of Homes in Category
7	4
8	5
9	5
10	10
11	6
12	4
13	3
15	2
Total	39

Since a great deal has been written about overcrowding in low income families, I next analyzed the data to determine the number of bedrooms in the various homes. As demonstrated in Table 4, the families in Golden Towers had three to six bedrooms: 158 residents occupied 152 bedrooms in thirty-nine households, which indicates an average of 1.04 persons per bedroom. When the number of bedrooms was further considered in relation to household composition, it is shown that the largest number of residents lived in four bedroom homes, that those bedrooms had an average of almost one person (.99). These

72

findings indicate that, unlike many black low income homes in the black subsociety, the bedrooms in Golden Towers were not overcrowded. Moreover, with one exception, there were never more than two people in a bedroom and, in a majority of the bedrooms, there was one or no persons. Though the residents were not asked whether spouses slept in the same room, as far as I could determine, at least a majority of husbands and wives slept together.

TABLE 4

Household Composition by Number of Bedrooms
in Golden Towers

Number of Bedrooms	Household Composition								No. of Homes	No. of Bedrooms	Total People
	2	3	4	5	6	7	8	9			
3	4	2	4	1	1		1		13	39	49
4	1	6	6	5	1				19	76	75
5	1	2		1		1			5	25	20
6				1				1	2	12	14
Total	6	10	10	8	2	1	1	1	39	152	158

Besides the census type data about the physical setting of homes in Golden Towers, I was also interested in the uses of rooms. I found that all the rooms were multi-purpose settings. Starting with the kitchen, it was not only used as a place to cook, talk, and eat, but it was also a gathering place for family and close friends, informal meetings, sewing, studying, doing the laundry, watching television, and writing letters. Another room was the den: It was also a setting for eating snacks, entertaining guests, holding prayer meetings, listening to records, playing cards, practicing piano lessons, reading, relaxing, sewing, sleeping, studying, playing, typing, and watching television. Similarly, the family room was used as a family meeting place for eating, meetings, parties, playing games, playing the piano, reading, rolling hair, sewing, napping, studying, talking, typing, and watching television. The difference between the den and family room was seen mainly in size and decoration; hence, the family room was usually larger and had more elaborate furnishings than the den.

The bedrooms were also multi-purpose rooms. They were used for doing paper work, entertaining, exercising, listening to music, playing, reading, relaxing, sewing, studying, talking, telephoning, watching television, praying, and sleeping.

The living room and dining areas were sometimes combined in the same room, while at other times, the dining area was a formal dining room. Unfortunately, I did not always make such distinction in my data; nevertheless, this area-room was used for eating, talking, displaying jewelry, playing cards, and sewing while the living room was used for entertaining guests, family entertainment, and piano practice.

Since twenty-one of the thirty-one homes in the home inventory sample had basements, I analyzed the data dealing with their uses. In five of the twenty-one basements, there were bedrooms, two of them had a kitchen, and an undetermined number of basements was the location for utility, laundry, and furnace rooms; in all cases, three excepted, the basement was also a recreational center. It was used as a setting for seated luncheons, dances, parties, receptions, fashion shows, games, relaxation, and television.

Since the data suggested that a number of rooms in the Golden Towers homes were used for leisure purposes, I abstracted those rooms, from the data, and found that leisure time pursuits take place in eight types of rooms in Golden Towers (see Table 5). They were the setting for eating, family activities, reading, parties, and relaxation. With considerable attention to leisure time space, I also became interested in the daily ritual that goes on in these rooms as well as in the rest of the home, a subject we will return to in Chapter 7.

TABLE 5

Leisure Time Rooms in Golden Towers

Types of Rooms	Number of Homes in Category
Breakfast	8
Cocktail	2
Den	16
Dining room/Area	39
Family Room	25
Living Room	39
Recreational Room	22
Study-Library	8

After determining that there was variation in the number of rooms in the Golden Towers homes, as well as the number of bedrooms and types of leisure time rooms, in my opinion, the next important question these data raised was why was there variation in house sizes. As seen in Table 6, I attempted to answer this question by looking at the occupational affiliation of spouses. As shown, there was no clear pattern, for blue collar men had homes in each size category; perhaps the most vivid pattern was that housewives lived in homes with ten, eleven, thirteen, and fifteen rooms. What this indicates is that housewives were usually married to men whose occupational earnings were relatively substantial. However, when I found that the occupational variable was not a significant indicator of the number of rooms in the homes, I turned next to my first hunch, income. As seen in Table 7, income is related to number of rooms in the household: thus spouses in seven room homes earn the lowest annual income while spouses in homes with eleven or more rooms earn the highest annual income. Though it is clear that number of rooms in homes is directly related to amount of annual income, I shall take this interpretation a step further. Thus, I also concluded that, more than any other factor, the number of rooms in black middle class homes is usually a function of their economic situation, at the time of the home purchase or construction. Assuming that this observation is correct, when some families settled in Golden Towers, they likely experienced a different economic situation than the remainder of the families. What can happen in such situation is that the economic gap can get larger, remain stable, or get smaller: it is my opinion that, in Golden Towers, all three patterns were evident.

TABLE 6

Number of Rooms and Occupations
of Spouses in Golden Towers

Number of Rooms	Occupation of Husband			Occupation of Wife			House-Wife
	Blue Collar	White Collar	Profes-sional	Blue Collar	White Collar	Profes-sional	
7	1	1	1	1		3	
8	1	3	1	1	2	2	
9	3	1			1	4	
10	4	3	3	1	2	6	1
11	1	2	3		3		3
12	1	1	2			4	
13	2	3				3	2
15	1		1				2
Total	14	14	11	3	8	22	8

TABLE 7

Number of Rooms and Household Income
in Golden Towers

Number of Rooms	Household Income
7	12,000 - 19,999
8	15,000 - 24,999
9	17,000 - 19,999
10	10,000 - 24,999
11	12,000 - Over 50,000
12	17,000 - 49,999
13	17,000 - Over 50,000
15	Reportedly 1/2 Millionairess and a Millionaire

Furnishings.

Before beginning the inventory of the home furnishings, as mentioned earlier, I received training in the recognition of furniture styles from the Home Advisory Department in an Atlanta department store. One of the Home Advisory representatives conceptualized traditional furnishings for this study as furniture that is more personable than other styles and that has excellent workmanship and fine, graceful, and elegant lines. It was also seen as period furniture, such as that which originated in the fourteenth, fifteenth, and sixteenth centuries, including Louis XIV furniture with carving on its legs, Louis XV with curved legs, and Louis XVI furniture with fluted legs. Of course, in includes much more, such as painted and unpainted French Provincial, Chippendale, Queen Anne, and Early American styles, and its fabric is soft in color and the skirts to its sofas usually extend to the floor. On the other hand, The Home Advisory representative conceptualized contemporary furnishings, for this study, as pieces of furniture that are crisp and express sleek, clean, and straight lines. It also, he continued, has bold colors and large round or square shapes and lacks ornamentation; besides, it gives one a feeling of spaciousness and openness. The Home Advisory representative next conceptualized an eclectic room. He told me that it had a mixture of traditional and contemporary furnishings and offers a contrast to either type of room. Such a room, he continued, has an individual look that can take on one of several appearances, a very cluttered look, an organized cluttered look, a clean graceful look, or a sophisticated look. Then, he warned me that one piece of traditional or contemporary furniture is not sufficient to give the eclectic effect, for there must be a good mixture of traditional and contemporary furniture. Using these descriptions, the representative and I identified, in his department, the different types of furnishings that he had conceptualized.

With the preparation that was given, gratis, by the Home Advisory Department, I began making inventories of furnishings in Golden Towers. Such inventories were taken while touring the homes, unless the residents objected. This experience occurred in three homes; hence, instead of taking notes, I memorized the furnishings and the decor in each room and went quickly home and typed the report. It should be mentioned, however, that after I completed the inventory, in three homes, I returned to the Home Advisory Department for a second session to determine the accuracy of the inventory data. When the inventory process was completed, I had an enormous amount of information about each room in the thirty-one homes. Since the foyer, the living room, and the master bedroom were the most elaborate rooms in the homes, they provided more ethnographic data. Consequently, they are used here to describe the physical setting in the households in Golden Towers.

The Foyer.

I found that twenty-one of the thirty-one homes had foyers; of that number, sixteen had a traditional decor, four were contemporary, and one was eclectic. The sixteen traditional foyers were furnished and decorated as follows:

1. Queen Anne bench and mirror and a green antique vase

2. Gold ornated mirror above a Queen Anne bench and an artificial rose bush

3. Ornated mirror and bench

4. Ornated mirror above a Queen Anne bench and chandelier

5. Floral arrangement, French provincial chest, and desk

6. Arm chair, table, ornated vase on table, and an ornated mirror above table

7. Venetian mirror over an Italian console with marble top, blue vase with a pink floral arrangement on console, and a ribbed ceiling in the shape of a Pagoda

8. Ornated mirror and bench, six or seven foot artificial palm, antique vase, bookcase with great books, and wall to wall carpet

9. Ornate mirror hung above a French Provincial bench, a decorative plant, and wall to wall carpet

10. Two green tufted velvet chairs, trimmed in antique gold and white, an antique gold and white table with white marble top, and ornate mirror above table

11. Two hand made chairs, sent from Spain, and Oriental rug

12. French Provincial Lava Bowl and chirrups with floral arrangement

13. French Provincial chest

14. Queen Anne mirror and bench and chime clock

15. Long pier mirror hung over ornate bench, artificial palm and rose tree

16. Louis XIV table, marble vase with chirrups and pink and rose silk flowers on table, a Queen Anne mirror above table, a muffin stand, a Napolenic chandelier, and portraits of son

The four contemporary foyers were less elaborate than the traditional foyers. One included a table and floral arrangement, another had a mirror with a plain frame, the third foyer had a chandelier, floral tree, and pink carpet, and a list was not made of the furnishings in the fourth contemporary foyer. I did, however, take notes on the eclectic foyer: it had a contemporary mirror, artificial plant, wall to wall carpet, a traditional credenze, and decorative vase.

The Living Room.

The next room that comprises the sample of rooms is the living room. When they were categorized, on the basis of furniture style, I found that twenty-one were traditional, seven were contemporary, and three were eclectic. Because it would take too much space to include a description of all the living rooms in the sample, by giving each one a number and by using a table of random numbers, I randomly selected one traditional living room. This living room, a more elaborate living room, and a dining room inventory will now be used to describe these settings.

Furnishing Inventories By Rooms

Living Rooms

1. A Randomly Selected Living Room

Pieces of Furniture	Style of Furniture	Quality of Furniture
1. Sofa	French Provincial	All pieces very
2. Love Seat	French Provincial	good quality
3. Two arm chairs	Traditional	
4. Coffee table (coral-hand-painted)	Traditional	
5. Side table	French Provincial	
6. Lamp with prisms	Contemporary	

Draperies

Pink with cornice

Floor Covering

Wall to wall carpet

2. A More Elaborate Living Room

Pieces of Furniture	Style of Furniture	Quality of Furniture
1. Louis XIII Love Seat	Traditional	Excellent
2. Louis XIV Sofa	Traditional	
3. Two Louis XIV tables with marble tops		
4. Two Louis XIV Side chairs	Traditional	
5. French Provincial Coffee Table	Traditional	
6. Louis XIV Side Table	Traditional	
7. Louis XIII Sofa	Traditional	

Dining Area/Room

1. A Dining Area

Pieces of Furniture	Style of Furniture	Quality of Furniture
1. Dining table (Queen Anne)	Traditional	Excellent
2. Six chairs (Queen Anne)	Traditional	
3. Chandelier	Traditional	
4. China cabinet (Queen Anne)	Traditional	
5. Two bronze pedestals	Traditional	

6. Two chirrups with greenery	Traditional	

Draperies

Swags were like the ones in the living-room -- because the living and dining room were enclosed in the same wall space.

Floor Covering

Wall to wall carpet

2. A Dining Room

Pieces of Furniture	Style of Furniture	Quality of Furniture
1. Table and four chairs that have red velvet upholstery	Antique	Excellent
2. Two chairs	Antique	
3. Chandelier	Traditional	
4. Floral arrangement of roses on table		
5. China Cabinet	Antique	
6. Marble Top Buffet	Antique	
7. Server - with a Civil Server Set display	Traditional	

Draperies

Green and white draperies with sheers	Traditional	

Wall Coverings

1. Bronze sculpture
   picture

2. Three pictures   Traditional
   (fruit and flowers)

Floor Coverings

Wall to wall floral design carpet

Master Bedroom

The next room to be described in this sample is the master bedroom. Of the twenty-nine women who permitted me to make an inventory of the furnishings in this room, sixteen of them had a traditional motif in their master bedroom, twelve had a contemporary decor, and one had an eclectic arrangement. Using a table of random numbers, a traditional bedroom, along with a more elaborate bedroom with a traditional decor, was selected to describe master bedrooms with such decor.

Master Bedrooms

1. A Randomly Selected Master Bedroom

Pieces of Furniture	Style of Furniture	Quality of Furniture
1. Bed	Early American	Quality is Good Plus
2. Dresser	Early American	
3. Chest	Early American	
4. Night Stand	Early American	

2. A More Elaborate Master Bedroom

Pieces of Furniture	Style of Furniture	Quality of Furniture
1. Bed	Colonial	Excellent

Pieces of Furniture	Style of Furniture	Quality of Furniture
2. Dresser	Colonial	
3. Chest	Colonial	
4. Lamp	Traditional	
5. Night Stand	Traditional	
6. Shell Chair		
7. Chair	Queen Anne	
8. Arm Chair	Traditional	

Draperies

The draperies are white with white rose designs

Floor Covering

Wall to wall carpet

Wall Covering

1. Mirror	Traditional	
2. Picture of hands in a prayful position	Traditional	

Interpretation of Findings.

The findings in this study seem to suggest a number of implications about black middle class homes in Golden Towers. One such implication is that the homes support Mead's (1958) view that the ideal situation in the American middle class is where each child has its own room, as well as Chapman's (1955) finding in Liverpool that middle class homes have a number of rooms, and Goffman's (1951) view of conformity in the middle class, for the homes in Golden Towers had basically the same decor and types of rooms; and they were used the same way. However, a related finding was that there was also a great deal of variation in lot sizes and number of rooms.

Another related implication in this study was that the number of rooms in homes was a function of economic status, a finding supported by Chapman (1955:16). And similar to Mead's (1958) suggestion about the home as "a sort of stage set," in Golden Towers, families, especially the women, when they entertained, used the home as a stage where they displayed their taste in clothing, food, furnishings, silver, china, crystal, and linen, and exquisite gifts to winners of bridge games as well as husbands' assistance with social occasions. However, the home in Golden Towers was not only a stage, it was also a dominant symbol of middle class status.

A related implication of these findings is that the foyer, living and dining rooms, and the basements were mainly areas that symbolized such social status while the kitchen, breakfast rooms, bedrooms, dens, family rooms, and cocktail rooms were utilitarian areas as well as symbols of social status. Perhaps their location in the homes also support this observation, for the foyers, living rooms, and dining rooms were located at the front of the homes where they were easily seen: other types of rooms were located either near the back of the home or on another floor.

These findings suggests another implication that relates to the front of the home as opposed to its back. Hence, it is concluded that the back of the home is used more than the front. Besides, these findings have some implications about the frequency of using various floors and, as seen in Figure 1, Golden Towers is predominantly a one floor neighborhood, which means that most activity went on not only toward the back of the home, but also on the ground floors. Another related implication is that, though basements served a number of uses, a majority of them were rarely used. A final implication concerns uses of rooms and, as shown in this paper, there was a great deal of use duplicaton in various rooms and, in part, it may mean that when it comes to leisure time at home, a number of settings may be needed to help the Golden Towers residents unwind from the day's work, and/or they need reassurance of their middle class status. This duplicity, however, may also be an indication of something else about the black middle class family. It may suggest, for example, a great deal of individuality, social independence, and differential leisure time preferences or television shows, which is what I often found among young siblings, or it may represent conformity to standards of their status (Goffman, 1951).

In conclusion, then, this study seems to tell a great deal about the black middle class family in Golden Towers. It provides information about their taste in home styles and furnishings as well as about the settings where their behavior takes place.

§§§§§§

NOTES

1. Margaret Mead. "The Contemporary Family As An Anthropologist Sees It. AMERICAN JOURNAL OF SOCIOLOGY, 1948, 53:458.

2. **Ibid.**

3. Dennis Chapman. THE HOME AND SOCIAL STATUS. New York: Grove Press, 1955. p. 17. Irving Goffman. "Symbols of Class Status" BRITISH JOURNAL OF SOCIOLOGY, II, 4 (December 1951).

4. **Ibid.**

CHAPTER SEVEN

RITUAL AND FOOD IN HOUSEHOLDS

Ritual is one type of behavior in the Golden Towers households. Although it has been a subject for research in religion and anthropology, it has been neglected in the modern family, especially in the black family, and food in the black household has only been a subject for research in dietetics. As a result, this chapter deals with the function of food patterns and ritual in Golden Towers. Following the authority of Bossard and Boll, ritual is conceptualized here as a "social process, with definite forms of interaction and a specific cultural content."[1] This discussion, therefore, emphasizes the daily activities[2] of the residents in Golden Towers.

The Awakening, School and Work Preparation and Leaving the House Ritual

A day was begun in Golden Towers with the awakening ritual. The spouses awakened before the children, either naturally or with the aid of a radio or an alarm clock. They began awakening between four and five-fifteen in the morning, but the largest percentage of the spouses awakened between five-thirty and six forty-five.

The awakening process was followed by the work and school preparation ritual. It consisted of bathing, showering, dressing, performing household and school tasks, and eating breakfast. Of course, a few individuals, in several households, and some entire households, did not eat a morning meal while in others the family members either ate a continental breakfast or a full meal. However, regardless of amount of food, family members usually ate breakfast in relays.

Following breakfast, the majority of the Golden Towers families participated in the leaving the house ritual. The men began leaving for work between six and seven o'clock, while the women started leaving between seven and eight o'clock in the morning. However, the largest number of the men left home between seven and nine o'clock, and the largest number of women left home between seven and eight o'clock.

Because ritual is conceptualized here as a "social process, with definite forms of interaction and a specific cultural content," it appears that the neighborhood setting is a form of ritual. Over the ten month period of fieldwork, there were a number of patterns and variations in the physical setting. It was seen that, while the residents were at work, the homes were surrounded by immense silence and that draperies were closed in practically all homes, except where they were left open in the living, kitchen, and family rooms; and, even then, the sheers often gave a closed appearance.

The Daily Ritual of Housewives.

Though the male and female residents in Golden Towers were an employed population, there were seven full time and three part-time housewives. They sometimes got lonely and looked for companionship and ways to contribute to their families and community. One widow, for example, took a hot cooked meal daily to her invalid kinsmen and spent a good portion of the remainder of the day on the telephone with him while another housewife engaged in a variety of volunteer activities. She volunteered her services, to her Links Organization (a nationally organized social and civic group of women who often help make up the highest socioeconomic level in the American black subsociety) and represented them, before a Georgia State Legislative Committee, concerning the inclusion of black history in textbooks and courses. She also atended meetings of the Metropolitan Housing Commission, League of Women's Voters, a theatrical arts committee, and social clubs. Besides, all the housewives shopped, visited their kinsmen and friends, and watched television, relaxed, prepared the family dinner, and did household chores.

The Dinner Hour Ritual.

Following work and school or daily activities at home, the dinner ritual took place. The members of each family usually ate dinner together. When a spouse or child had an assignment or activity that kept him away from home, at the regular dinner hour, the meal was sometimes delayed. Another ritualistic aspect of the meal was that it was eaten daily in the same room (usually in the kitchen) at dining bars or on round, oval, or rectangular tables.

The coming to the table ritual was the initial aspect of the meal. By the time that their plates had either been served from the stove or the food had been placed on the table, parents and children were expected to be seated at the table. One afternoon, for example, a wife rang the dinner bell, as was her customary practice, and the children ignored it by continuing to do their homework. Then she rang it again and, when they did not appear at the table, she told them they knew that the first bell meant to get ready for the meal (wash their hands) and that the second bell meant for them to be seated at the table.

The next aspect of the meal was the seating ritual. It was customary for each member of the family to have a permanent seat. The men sat at the head and the women sat either at the foot or on the sides of the table. A major consideration in the selection of a wife's seat was convenience to the stove. This was necessary because she was often the last person to be seated and sometimes served the family additional food. Although a child sometimes sat at the foot, the usual position of children, at the table, was on its sides. When the family ate at a bar, the father and mother usually sat next to each other and the children sat in front of them. Therefore, in a majority of cases, the parental generation could be separated from that of the children by their positions at the dinner table. Besides, similar to children, kinsmen in the home usually sat on the sides of the table.

Once the family was seated, the giving thanks ritual took place. This means that, prior to eating, the family members usually said Grace and, in one household, the husband said the Grace and each family member, in reverent and orderly succession, said a Bible verse. Following grace, the eating ritual was comprised of varied types of food and usually included a meat, two vegetables, and sometimes a salad. The women, with few exceptions, enjoyed preparing large, attractive, and tasty meals, and their husbands took pride in their culinary skills. Of course, some women had not developed their cooking skills and their spouses did a great deal of the cooking, especially on their days off while, in some cases, wives and their spouses shared the cooking.

Conversation was the next aspect of the dinner ritual and, starting with matters pertaining to children, it had at least two phases. The children related the nature of their daily events and reported their problems. by questioning, parents fitted their entire daily puzzle together and taught their children how to deal with similar problems in the future. Another phase of dinner conversation was parent dominated. It permitted them to teach their children about their occupations; one husband, for example, used the dinner hour to teach his sons about his garage business. Moreover, a few spouses, especially women, discussed discrimination problems encountered at work.

The length of time the families spent at the dinner table was also ritualized. The largest number of spouses spent either thirty or forty-five minutes at the table, and one and one-half hours were the longest time spent at the dinner table. A husband who spent the longest time at the table had a college education, a white collar job, and earned between $10,000 and approximately $14,000 dollars per annum. On the other hand, another husband who spent the same amount of time at the dinner table had elementary training and was employed in a blue collar occupation and earned approximately the same amount of money. On the other hand, the women who spent one and one-half hours at the dinner table had college training and white collar occupations and earned either between $2,000 to $6,000 dollars or between $10,000 and approximately $14,000 dollars annually. Because many other similar residents and those with doctorates and masters degrees did not use this much time at the dinner table, it was likely that additional factors, including schedules, television shows, household chores, varied other interests, and extent of family communication helped determine how long a family remained at the table.

Food.

A great deal has been written about the nutrition of low income blacks, and it has been found that their nutritive intake is often adequate. For example, Koh and Caples found in 250 low income Black households in Claiborne, Mississippi that the "Nutrient intake was low for a substantial number of the subjects," especially adolescents.[3] It was also found in a 541 population survey in southwestern Mississippi, that "a substantial proportion of the persons had a low caloric intake,"[4] a finding supported in a subsequent study made by Haider and Wheeler.[5]

There are also certain food buying practices among low income blacks; hence, in 76.1 percent of a sample, in southwestern Mississippi, it was found that there is "A lack of concern for nutrition when buying food" and that food was based primarily on taste preference in 42.3 percent of the families while 25.8 percent based their food selection on nutritional value.[6] In a related study, Wheeler and Haider found among ghetto blacks and Hispanics in Brooklyn that mothers planned their meals "only one day at a time" and that they prepared "fried food most often and broiled least often."[7] On the other hand, Brittin and Zinn found in Lubbock, Texas that "the amount and cost of pork sausage were greater for Negroes" than for Mexican-Americans and Caucasins.[8] Reaburn et al. somewhat placed the food patterns of low income blacks in perspective when they noted that "availability, convenience, price, and prestige were the parameters used in studying the use of fifty-two foods by low income homemakers"[9] while Steelman suggested that the meaning and significance of food can be better understood when it is seen in "relationship to the total life styles of individuals and groups."[10] The findings suggest that, though the diet of low income blacks is inadequate, it is varied.

The food intake in Golden Towers supported the observation that Blacks eat a variety of food. Nevertheless, at dinner time, there is an observable food pattern. The three most frequently eaten meats, for example, in this order, were chicken, beef, and steak while the least frequently eaten meats were pork chops, lamb, ham, and pork ribs. These findings indicate that the residents in Golden Towers ate more poultry and beef than pork, which may contribute to less high blood pressure.

The residents also ate a wide variety of vegetables, but there were six that were eaten most often. In this order, they included turnips, snap beans, collards, garden peas, squash, and broccoli; however, a great deal of other food was also served at dinner. The food patterns in Golden Towers also contributed to the festive nature of the dinner hour, unless, of course, a family member had a problem. In such case, the entire family was involved in its resolution.

When the most frequently eaten meat, poultry, and the most frequently eaten vegetable, turnips, were crosstabulated with education, occupation, and income, there were no significant differences. What this suggests, is that food patterns in these black middle class households were relatively homogeneous. These findings also suggest that, though black middle class families in Golden Towers eat some pork, they eat less pork than has been the case in black families below the middle class.

The food patterns in Golden Towers were even more vivid when the women entertained their bridge clubs or when they entertained dinner guests. On such occasions, large meals were served, and each woman had at leat one favorite menu. For example, the favorite menu of a professional wife was home baked rolls, tossed salad, cartwheel candied yams, sprinkled with crushed pineapple, roast beef, baby peas, okra, sliced pickled beets, and homemade strawberry cream pie with pink champagne. One of the favorite dinner menus that a white collar wife enjoyed serving guests was a twelve hour hickory smoked turkey with fiesta rice dressing, whole baby squash, whole string beans, and congealed salad, followed with coffee, dessert, and liqueur. While serving their guests, a majority of the women used fine china, silver, and crystal.

Anticipating these food and service patterns, another question on the structured interview schedule asked the women whether they had learned any behavior from whites that they were using or may use in the future. A variety of responses was given, but the ones that related to this topic were that they had been given new recipes and taught to improve their cooking skills and how to entertain. The white collar wife, whose menu we identified, answered this question thusly:

> I received my entertainment inspiration from wealthy white women and they taught me how to entertain. For example, my mother served as housekeeper for one wealthy white woman whose manners I liked. That is, she was very lady-like, and a perfect hostess who used fine silver, china, and linen at meal time. It was my goal to be like her.

Judging by the home setting and entertainment style, this Golden Towers resident appears to be approaching her goal.

After Dinner Ritual.

Following the dinner hour, the families participated in varied rituals, including recreation. The adults attended voluntary association meetings, visited friends and relatives, entertained, watched television, did school work, and helped with household chores, including washing dishes.

The last activity in the evening was the going to bed ritual. Although children usually went to bed between eight o'clock and midnight, their most popular bedtime hour was between nine and ten o'clock. Though some adults also went to bed between eight and nine o'clock, a majority of them got in bed between eleven and one o'clock. The going to bed ritual included varied activities, including praying. One husband, for example, said his prayers before getting in bed and, during his many years of marriage, he had prayed on his knees nightly. When he had a few drinks, his prayer ritual was delayed; he went to bed, snoozed a little, awakened, got up, prayed, and went back to sleep; the prayer ritual was customary in this home, especially when trouble loomed. Once spouses got in bed, a number of other activities ensued, such as reading, sewing, and writing.

The Weekend Ritual.

The Saturday ritual differed from the remainder of the week, because during the day, family members went on household errands and performed household chores and, at night, they engaged in recreation, including playing family games and watching television. On the other hand, the Sunday ritual resembled the work week, for the first person got up at five o'clock and, at least one person, awakened in most homes between five and seven-thirty or between eight-thirty and nine o'clock. Of course, the time the families got up in the morning was often related to Sunday School and church attendance. A large number of the family members who got up early went to Sunday School and/or church while residents who did not go to church often slept or stayed in bed until midday or afternoon. Nevertheless, the women usually awakened first and were responsible for awakening the remainder of the family and cooking and serving the Sunday morning meal between eight and ten thirty o'clock or after the family returned from church. It followed, then, that for some families, the church going ritual was the next major Sunday activity; however, the residents spent varying amounts of time in church.

On Sunday afternoon, for all families, the relaxation ritual was the dominant activity. To demonstrate this point, Father's Day, 1970, will be described. In the "Woodsons'" home, the husband rested in bed, a son relaxed in a chair, another son and nephew shopped for a Father's Day gift, and the wife cooked the Sunday dinner and, though she usually served her husband's dinner in bed, because he worked long hours in the family business, the entire family ate in the dining room. Later in the afternoon, the draperies were closed in all rooms and, apparently, family members who remained at home went to sleep. Similarly in the "Pelts'" home, the wife slept in the bedroom while her husband slept in the family room, but the "Lowell's" household included slightly more activity, for the mother and daughter talked and cooked dinner while the son played with his toys, and the father, a public school music teacher, spent the afternoon reading and listening to classical music and rarely engaged in conversation. A wedding reception was held in another home; and at the "Lees'" home, a husband and wife entertained their friends from another section of Atlanta. The activity inside the homes surpassed what was happening outside, for only three boys, riding motor bikes, were seen in the streets. Thus, as a rule, the Golden Towers residents spent Sunday afternoon shopping, visiting, eating out, cooking, listening to music, watching television, sleeping, reading, and entertaining.

Implications of Findings.

The purpose of this chapter was to determine the function of food patterns and ritual in Atlanta black households. the primary function of the early morning ritual was to get family members to their jobs and schools. On the other hand, the daily ritual of housewives functioned to counteract or prevent loneliness and with only a couple of exceptions, housewives, on all socioeconomic levels, engaged in the same daily activities. Perhaps the dinner hour ritual performed more functions, for the household, than any other ritual. For example, it functioned to teach disciplining and religious behavior and to separate the child and parental generations while merging the grandchild and grandparental generations. The dinner ritual also functioned as an outlet for discussion and resolution of personal problems and as a time for fun and relaxation. And it does not appear that socioeconomic factors were significantly related to length of time spent at the table and type of food eaten. However, it appears that, unlike low income families, nutritious and well prepared meals were symbolic of black middle class status. Besides, after dinner and work ritual functioned to provide opportunities for family relaxation and participation in voluntary associations.

It is thus concluded that food and ritual in Golden Towers households served a number of functions related to employment, social status, amelioration of loneliness, and possibly improved health and family relations, especially husband and wife behavior.

NOTES

1. James Bossard and Eleanor S. Boll. RITUAL IN FAMILY LIVING. Philadelphia: University of Pennsylvania Press, 1950, p. 16.

2. **Ibid.**, p. 17.

3. Eunsook T. Koh and Virginia Caples. "Nutrient Intake of Low-Income black Families in Southwestern Mississippi." JOURNAL OF THE AMERICAN DIETETIC ASSOCIATION. Vol. 75, 1979, p. 669.

4. **Ibid.**, p. 666.

5. Sanober Q. Haider and Madeleine Wheeler. "Dietary Intake of Low Socioeconomic Black and Hispanic Teenage Girls." JOURNAL OF AMERICAN DIETETIC ASSOCIATION. Vol. 77, 1980, p. 680.

6. Eunsook T. Koh and Virginia Caples. "Frequency of Selection of Food Groups by Low-Income Families in Southwestern Mississippi." JOURNAL OF THE AMERICAN DIETETIC ASSOCIATION. Vol. 74, 1979, p. 661.

7. Madeleine Wheeler and Sanober Q. Haider. "Buying and Food Preparation Patterns of Ghetto Blacks and Hispanics in Brooklyn." JOURNAL OF THE AMERICAN DIETETIC ASSOCIATION. Vol. 75, 1979, p. 562.

8. Helen C. Britten and Dale W. Zinn. "Meat Buying Practices of Caucasians, Mexican-Americans, and Negroes." JOURNAL OF THE AMERICAN DIETETIC ASSOCIATION. Vol. 71, 1977, p. 627.

9. Janice A. Reaburn et al. "Social Determinants in Food Selection." AMERICAN DIETETIC ASSOCIATION JOURNAL. Vol. 74, 1979, p. 637.

10. Virginia Purtle Steelman. "Attitudes Toward Food as Indicators of Subcultural Value Systems." HOME ECONOMICS RESEARCH JOURNAL. Vol., 5, 1976, p. 32.

CHAPTER EIGHT

BLACK HUSBANDS AND WIVES:
AN ASSESSMENT OF MARITAL ROLES IN
A MIDDLE-CLASS NEIGHBORHOOD

Studies of the black family have primarily focused on the low income and working class communities. Matrifocality, conceptualized as "close affective ties, domestic units dominated by females, and high frequencies of households" (Otterbein, 1966, p. vii), is one type of family structure found in the lower class family (Frazier, 1939, pp. 102-113; Hippler, 1974, p. 47; Moynihan, 1967, pp. 30-31; and Powdermaker, 1962, p. 204). In the Hunter's Point study by Hippler, such households were described as headed either by a grandmother whose daughters and grandchildren lived with her or by a mother whose children lived with her (Hippler, 1974, p. 21). The female heads were central figures and the only financial, emotional, and authority leaders in the household; in fact, the men were described as unsuited to steady employment (Hippler, 1974, pp. 43,47). Similarly, the men in a Syracuse, New York low rent housing project experienced a high rate of unemployment (Willie, 1967, pp. 137-138). The economic marginality of men in such settings as those described by Hippler and Willie tends to foster the maintenance of a black matriarchy. Moreover, it has been found that the black matriarchy in the lower class is a consequence of slavery (Frazier, 1939, p. 102) and more recently of the economic insecurity of Afro-American males (Hippler, 1974, p. 217; King, 1945, p. 103; Powdermaker, 1962, p. 205; and Smith, 1956, p. 22). The prevalence of a matriarchy, however, has been challenged by a number of writers. The Cromwells (1978, pp. 754-756), on the basis of their inner-city neighborhood sample in Kansas City, and Staples (1977, pp. 174-183), using a historical per-

---

Reprinted by permission of BLACK MARRIAGE AND FAMILY THER-
APY, Edited by Constance E. Obudho, Greenwood Press, Westport,
Connecticut, 1983.

spective, concluded that the concept of the black matriarchy must be rejected, for it is not the dominant relationship in the black family.

Patriarchy, another type of family structure associated with the black family, is seldom found in Afro-American lower-class communities. Patriarchy, however, has been seen in black working-class communities in Rivertown County, Missouri and Pulpwood County, Florida (Martin and Martin, 1978, p. 20). Furthermore, Scanzoni (1971, p. 241) found that in the American black family the higher the husband's occupational status, the more likely he will resolve conflict in his favor.

The third type of family structure in the black community is equalitarianism. It was found to be the norm in working-class marriages in an inner-city neighborhood in Kansas City (Cromwell and Cromwell, 1978, p. 757) and in Rivertown and Pulpwood Counties (Martin and Martin, 1978, p. 20). It was also a feature of family life in Texas (Bullock, 1941, pp. 29-30) and among middle-class spouses, "especially when both are employed" (Frazier, 1957, p. 331).

Varied types of interaction, including cooperation in the performance of house-related tasks, also characterize the family in the black community. When roles were performed in Rivertown and Pulpwood counties, a rigid division of labor occurred (Martin and Martin, 1978, p. 20), but men in Hunter's Point, it was found, did not usually help their wives (Hippler, 1974, p. 47).

Affective behavior comprises another type of family interaction in the black community. Although black spouses desire companionship, physical affection, and empathy from marriage (Scanzoni, 1971, p. 201), it was impossible for women in Hunter's Point to obtain deep emotional relations; instead, females denigrated male sexuality, and the men were sullenly indifferent to their women or resorted to bragging (Hippler, 1974, pp. 42 and 49). Furthermore, Bernard (1966, p. 98) has suggested that "the Negro wife suffers deprivation in all areas, but it is relatively less marked in the area of companionship and love than in those of income and understanding." The achievement of a strong marital bond has been described as difficult, because blacks on the same social level as whites receive fewer dollars and less job satisfaction (Scanzoni, 1971, pp. 205-209). Moreover, money, extramarital sex, and family problems result in the dissolution of some black marriages (Holloman and Lewis, 1978, p. 223). However, when the occupational, educational, and income status increases, marital cohesiveness does not improve in a corresponding manner (Scanzoni, 1971, p. 201). In addition, it is suggested that large numbers of black women are alienated from black men primarily because of the "acquisition of the colonizer's cultural values" (Staples, 1979, p. 25).

As can be seen from this review of the literature, there are "serious gaps in our knowledge of marriage and family among Negroes" (Bernard, 1966, p. ix). An even greater void exists in the literature of the black middle-class family, which may be a consequence of several factors, including the difficulty of studying middle-class blacks. It may also result from the phenomenon of lumping all blacks together and sometimes comparing them with the white middle class. This chapter, however, will focus on family structure, cooperation, and affection in a black middle class neighborhood, and a number of concepts previously employed to describe the lower class black family will be applied to the black middle class family. A related purpose of this chapter is to determine the influence of sex, education, occupation, and income on family structure, spousal cooperation, and spousal affective relations.

FINDINGS -- Authority Patterns.

Matriarchy. The data show that matriarchy was the decision-making pattern in 16 of the 41 Golden Towers households. Both spouses, however, occupied each of the 16 households, two excepted because of widowhood. The women made a majority of the decisions concerning their children, including discipline, health care, clothing, and food needs, and concerning economic matters, including payment of bills and savings. Another area of female domination was family activities, such as religious behavior. They decided when and where the family went to church; of course, a few husbands belong to a different church from their wives. Similarly, the women directed the family's social life; they planned the social occasions in the home, accepted invitations to dinners, parties, dances, and fashion shows, and selected their family friends. Some of these women met their friends prior to marriage while others were met later on their jobs, in their churches, and in other organizations. At least one woman, however, was tired of associating only with friends she had known more than 20 years and wanted her husband to initiate new friendships. The men made friends on their jobs, but often they were not acceptable for joint social life (a consequence of their marital, social, or sex status). Of course, a few men made friends for their family.

Although the women were leaders in the matriarchal households, the men were not completely outside the decision making process. They had greater authority than their wives concerning the upkeep of their homes and lawns, spending large sums of money, purchase of cars, and vacation and recreational time schedules. However, as a rule, their authority was only exercised after the situation had been discussed with their spouses.

To set the matriarchal households in their proper perspective, the 16 women's views of the decision-making process was sought. It was not by choice that the women made decisions; in fact, they complained and argued with their spouses, because they did not think ahead for the family, take care of legal and financial business, and assume more household responsibility.

Another measurement utilized to determine the proper perspective of the matriarchal family was the influence of socioeconomic factors, including education, on decision making. As can be seen from Table 1, these women were more highly educated than their spouses. Similar to education, as shown in Table 2, the women held more prestigious occupations than men, but the men earned more annual income than the women, a consequence of male employment in relatively good paying blue collar jobs as opposed to their wives' employment in lower-paying white collar and professional occupations (see Table 3).

TABLE 1

Type of Household Authority by Education of Spouses in Golden Towers, 1970

	Type of Authority											
Education	Female						Male					
	Matriarchy		Patriarchy		Equalitarianism		Matriarchy		Patriarchy		Equalitarianism	
	N	%	N	%	N	&	N	%	N	%	N	%
Doctoral	0	0.0	2	22.2	0	0.0	0	0.0	3	33.3	3	18.7
Masters	7	43.7	0	0.0	6	37.5	1	7.1	1	11.1	1	6.3
College	6	37.5	6	66.7	10	62.5	8	57.1	2	22.2	8	50.0
High School	1	6.3	1	11.1	0	0.0	2	14.3	3	33.3	3	18.7
Elem. School	2	12.5	0	0.0	0	0.0	3	21.4	0	0.0	1	6.3
Total	16	100.0	9	100.0	16	100.0	14	99.9	9	99.9	16	100.0

TABLE 2

Type of Household Authority by Occupation of Spouses in Golden Towers, 1970

	Type of Authority											
Occupation	Female						Male					
	Matriarchy		Patriarchy		Equalitarianism		Matriarchy		Patriarchy		Equalitarianism	
	N	%	N	%	N	%	N	%	N	%	N	%
Professional	8	50.0	5	55.6	11	68.8	2	14.3	3	33.3	7	43.7
White Collar	5	31.2	0	0.0	3	18.7	6	42.8	3	33.3	4	25.0
Blue Collar	0	0.0	0	0.0	0	0.0	6	42.8	3	33.3	5	31.3
Service Worker	1	6.3	1	11.1	0	0.0	0	0.0	0	0.0	0	0.0
Housewife	2	12.5	3	33.3	2	12.5	0	0.0	0	0.0	0	0.0
Total	16	100.0	9	100.0	16	100.0	14	99.9	9	99.9	16	100.0

TABLE 3

Type of Household Authority by Income of Spouses in Golden Towers, 1970

	Type of Authority											
Income	Female						Male					
	Matriarchy		Patriarchy		Equalitarianism		Matriarchy		Patriarchy		Equalitarianism	
	N	%	N	%	N	%	N	%	N	%	N	%
2,000- 5,999	1	16.7	1	50.0	3	23.1	0	0.0	0	0.0	1	8.3
6,000- 9,999	1	16.7	0	0.0	3	23.1	1	14.3	0	0.0	4	33.3
10,000-13,999	4	66.6	0	0.0	7	53.8	6	85.7	3	50.0	6	50.0
14,000- 17,999	0	0.0	0	0.0	0	0.0	0	0.0	0	0.0	0	0.0
22,000- 25,999	0	0.0	1	50.0	0	0.0	0	0.0	0	0.0	1	8.3
30,000- 49,999	0	0.0	0	0.0	0	0.0	0	0.0	1	16.7	0	0.0
50,000- 100,000	0	0.0	0	0.0	0	0.0	0	0.0	2	33.3	0	0.0
Total	6	100.0	2	100.0	13	100.0	7	100.0	6	100.0	12	99.9

Another reason for wife domination was that the men had experienced more job discrimination than women. This was seen in the length of time it took for them to prepare for their career. The women who were school teachers and school administrators utilized the usual training period, while a few of the men either did not receive all the training desired or spent twice as long preparing for their career. For example, one man was trained in cabinet making in the 1940's. Unable to obtain a job in cabinet making, he returned to college and earned a teaching degree. Although both sexes experienced difficulty getting promotions, the men had more problems than the women. The men, for example, were assigned a lower rating or position in government and private industry than their work level, and their promotion was usually delayed. The women have reaped the consequences of their husbands' job experiences. They created, the women say, men who often refuse to discuss their marital difficulties and/or demand an unrestrained and independent position in the home, which frees them from particular household responsibilities and domination by their wives. This sense of independence, however, decreases the men's prestige in the family, a likely source of male insecurity. These findings suggest yet another dimension of matriarchy, namely, control of household is not synonymous with domination of male spouse. In fact, the personal independence of the husband in some wife-dominated households puts him in a unique position in the black family. He has more personal autonomy than other men in the black family complex.

Although racial discrimination and the relatively low educational and occupational attainment levels of husbands in wife-dominated households are related to matriarchy, they do not adequately account for it since husbands in equalitarian and patriarchal households share the same experiences. It is likely that spouses develop during childhood, to varying degrees, the ability to receive and give love, ambition, leadership skills, and effective decision making. When parents, especially mothers, fail to teach these skills, here called the benign male socialization process, sons will be underprepared to contribute significantly to the family decision making process. Additionally, perhaps the extent to which childhood skills reach maturity is influenced by the socialization process experienced by the men's wives; a domineering wife could impede the man's development.

Patriarchy. Husband domination, another household relationship, is similar to matriarchal authority. In nine Golden Towers households, the men decided their schedule, approved the activities of their wives and children, and determined the use of household finances, but the women implemented a majority of their decisions and were responsible for the performance of household chores.

An attempt was also made to set patriarchy in its proper perspective by asking the women in these households their reactions. A few of them were subservient, while others desired to utilize their leadership potential; but those who adjusted best to their subservient roles experienced less stress and strain than women who showed dislike for them. Consequently, male domination may be related to female insecurity. The influence of socioeconomic factors was also utilized to set male dominance in its proper perspective. It was found that education (see Table 1) was significantly related to it. The highest percentage of men in the husband-dominated households had doctorate degrees and high school training, and decision making was not controlled by men who only had elementary training; but the women in husband-dominated households were more highly educated than the men. The men, however, had more prestigious occupations than their wives; hence, 66.6 percent were in white collar and professional positions, 33.0 percent were in blue collar positions, and there were no service work men in male-dominated households (see Table 2). On the other hand, 55.6 percent of their wives were in professional occupations, 11.1 percent were in service work, and 33.3 percent were housewives. A smaller percentage of women in husband-dominated than wife-dominated and equalitarian households worked. Additionally, it was found that all husbands who earned $30,000 or more per annum dominated their households, but there were three men who dominated their homes and earned between $10,000 and $13,999 annually (see Table 3). These findings suggest that childhood socialization, personal training, and a satisfactory self-concept enabled the men in the middle income range to control their households. Moreover, education, prestigious occupations, and enough income to support family were often basic to patriarchy.

Equalitarianism. This was the third type of husband and wife decision-making pattern in Golden Towers. Sixteen couples manifested equal control over household decisions. There was a lot of give and take, and the best suggestions were accepted. Sometimes, however, a spouse made decisions independently, but at times it had severe consequences. A husband, for example, surprised his working wife by giving her a new car for her birthday; she became ill and remained home from work three days.

An attempt was also made to set the equalitarian households in their proper persepctive by asking the couples their reaction to

103

the joint decision-making process. In varying degrees, their marriage relations were relaxed and satisfying. In fact, these couples were happier than the patriarchal and matriarchal couples. Moreover, not only did they make joint decisions, but there was no rigid division of labor in their implementation. To understand equalitarianism more fully, we correlated the socioeconomic characteristics of the spouses with the decision-making process. As can be seen from Table 1, the women in these households had bachelors and masters degrees while their spouses were represented unequally among elementary, high school, college, and graduate training. Nevertheless, 75 percent of the men had at least some college training. This seems to give additional support to the proposition that education is significant to effective participation in the household. It was also found that the women had more prestigious occupations than their spouses. Hence, 87.5 percent were in professional and white collar positions while 68.7 percent of their spouses were in the same occupations (see Table 2), and each spouse earned up to $13,999 annually, although one male exception earned up to $25,999 per annum (see Table 3). Since the women were ahead of their spouses educationally and occupationally and earned about the same income, it is likely that the male spouses' equal contribution to the household also resulted from a nonbenign socialization process during childhood. On the other hand, they may have taught themselves how to participate effectively in the household. Of course, some women say they taught their spouses the necessary household skills and knowledge. Moreover, equal earnings may sometimes help establish spousal equality in the home.

Cooperative Relations.

Although all the men may not dominate or participate on an equal basis with their wives in the decision-making process, some of them assist with house-related tasks, including shopping for groceries, cooking, setting the table, washing dishes, and house cleaning. To understand men's performance of household tasks, each chore was cross-tabulated with the education, occupation, and income status of the men. It was consistently found that men who either had some college training or a college degree, blue collar occupations, and earned an annual income between $10,000 and $13,999 performed household tasks more often than the other men. Since six blue collar husbands were married to women in professional occupations, and three were married to women in white collar positions, assistance with household chores may be one way they enhanced their status in the home. Moreover, it is likely that men who occupy the highest and lowest educational, occupational, and income status consider housework demeaning to their manhood. Another index employed to provide understanding of men's domestic chores was the employment of their spouse. The husbands whose spouses were either full or part-time housewives were excerpted to determine whether or not the husbands performed household chores less frequently than husbands whose wives worked. All husbands of the seven full-time and three part-time wives performed at least one of the household tasks, but less frequently and for varied reasons. Thus, husbands shopped for groceries and cooked for such reasons as they had flexible schedules, and their wives had not developed their culinary skills. This analysis, therefore, suggests that the husbands of housewives do fewer house-related tasks than men whose wives work. Interestingly, husbands of these women were 40 to 69 years old, had an educational level that ranged from fourth grade to doctorate degrees, worked in professional, white collar, and blue collar occupations, and earned from $10,000 to approximately $100,000 annually. On the other hand, they were married to women who were 30 to 69 years of age and had either a college degree or some college or elementary school education.

Expressive Relations.

Expressive behavior, conceptualized as congenial conversation, companionship, use of names to address spouse, and emotional satisfaction, is another type of spousal behavior. The couples' conversation spanned varied topics, one being previous employment. A college-educated man recounted to his wife his earlier life when he worked hard on the farm for a small amount of money, clothing, or animal manure, which he later sold. Perhaps, this is one way he reinforced the extent of his social mobility. Conversation also focused on their contact with whites at professional, civic, and political meetings, and in graduate schools and about racial discrimination, segregation, job experiences, card playing, their children, and their antebellum ancestors. Moreover, the women talked about what they had taught white women and what they had learned from them. Of course, some of the women said they had not learned anything from whites they planned to use.

Companionship, the next type of expressive behavior between spouses, included giving parties, visiting their kinsmen, riding, fishing, playing bridge and other games, watching television, dancing, and attending social and religious activities. Ocasionally, a few spouses attended the opera and symphony.

The names spouses used to address one another provided a closer view of their emotional relationship. The men employed a larger number (9) of term categories than the women (7) to address their spouses. However, the largest number addressed their spouses by their first name and, unlike the women, there were no men who called their wives by their last name. Furthermore, as many men (9) as women (10) utilized an endearing term to address their spouse: five used only an endearing concept, while four alternated between the use of an endearing concept and a first name or nickname. The men's endearing concepts for their wives were Sweetheart, Sugar, Darling, Darling Dear, Sweetie Face, Baby, Big Angel, and Hon. On the other hand, eight of the women called their spouses by his first name and four by his last name. It was the custom in the 1930's and early 1940's in some sections of the South for black women to be introduced to a man by his last name which they used until marriage. Once they were married, some of the spouses started calling each other by endearing concepts. When they began their family, they changed to Daddy, and when the children were grown, the women reverted to calling them by their last name. Some other women addressed their husbands by nicknames (5), and nickname and Daddy alternately (1), and Daddy (2). The latter was employed to teach young children what to call their father, but it also suggests a certain degree of closeness in the marital relationship. In addition, there were women who addressed their husbands by alternating between their first name and an endearing term (5) and by only an endearing term (5). The terms of endearment employed by some women for their spouses were Hon, Honey, Sweetie, Sweetie Pie, Baby, Sweetheart, and Sweets and were associated with the total marital complex. Hence, some women employed them to denote a strong emotional bond, while others utilized endearing terms for emphasis in conversation and to get and maintain their husband's attention. Moreover, when spouses were getting along, the women called their husbands by endearing terms, and when tensions existed they addressed them by their first names. Another consideration concerning the use of endearing terms relates to the location of the couple; thus, endearing concepts were usually employed in privacy, while the first name was utilized in situations external to the family. Moreover, terms of address between marriage partners were somewhat reciprocal, but more men (9) than women (6) called their spouses by a nickname.

Another area of expressive husband and wife behavior was emotional satisfaction viewed as respect, warmth, tenderness, and physical affection. As mentioned in the methodology, when only three of the Golden Towers spouses were willing to discuss their own marital bond, it was necessary to obtain their opinions about the strength of all middle-class marriages. A minority of the Golden Towers residents viewed black middle-class marriages as a strong relationship. A white collar husband, for example, believed that wives are lovely and must be caressed and treated sweetly and tenderly and should not be on an equal footing with men, especially when it comes to participation in the military and exposure to harsh language. In addition, a blue collar man, a professional woman, and a part-time housewife held that black middle-class spouses love each other.

Alternatively, a majority of the residents viewed black middle-class marriages as weak. One housewife related that the marital link is weak because the women are responsible for the household, and the children do not receive enough attention. Another professional wife attributed it to the status of the husband; he has been deprived of a good education and forced to work for less money than he needs to support his family. This becomes a source of marital stress. On the other hand, a professional man provided another dimension of marital problems. To him, marriages are weak because spouses are pulled in different directions; for example, variation in spousal occupational interests, religious dedication, and friendship types are a source of frustration for the women and their children. Moreover, in the opinion of a blue collar wife, the preceding marital problems are compounded by yet another dimension of marital behavior - extramarital relations. After a man achieves, she said, with the help of his wife, he gets outside interests and forgets about his home. Thus, although a wife may be in dire need of sex, some husbands leave their needs unfulfilled. Yet, an adequate sex life, she said, was crucial to husband and wife warmth.

That women in Golden Towers value warmth is evident. One woman, for example, related that "It is better to be able to show warmth toward another than to have a million dollars." Similarly, another wife related, "Warmth, love, or whatever you call it, keeps a life from being empty." Furthermore, all women would like their sons to demonstrate respect and kindness to black women, qualities that seem missing in some of their marriages. It appears, however, that some of the women who were either housewives, part-time housewives, or worked in non-authority-bearing and prestigious positions had the greatest need for a strong marital bond, but I hastily add that there were indeed women in authority-bearing and prestigious positions who were intensely interested in more love in their marriage. Additionally, these women talked incessantly about their jobs and children's achievements which, in part, may have been an unconscious effort to compensate for the emotional insecurity in their marriage relationship. It, therefore, seems safe to conclude that the intensity of need for more love and affection in marriage is related to individual needs and personality.

Of course, the extent of affection the women receive in marriage is likely to be related to their husband type. Judging by the women's comments and my own observations in Golden Towers, there seems to be three types of black men who become husbands. Type One is the insecure husband who needs to feel important to everybody, including his family and, therefore, centers his affections on himself. On the other hand, Type Two is the secure husband who has learned either during childhood or adulthood how to contribute effectively to the household and participate comfortably in its related activities. Moreover, he centers his affections on his family and himself and speaks kindly, a great deal of the time, to them. Type Three, however, is the split personality husband who also demands that his wife work; talks with her in a stiff, unsatisfying, and sometimes argumentative tone; yet is sometimes apologetic for his unkind behavior; expects his wife to forgive him quickly, and may or may not effectively assist with running the household. The types, however, are not rigid. Some black middle class husbands exhibit characteristics of each type. Perhaps Type Two, though, is the most desirable spouse; and from this analysis it appears that the safest way to develop Type Two is to start at birth. This requires women to train their sons in decision making, cooperation, and receiving and giving love in kin relations. It requires fathers and mothers to daily demonstrate these virtues. In addition, this training should be accompanied by educational and occupational preparation for earning a good living. Lastly, since black women have the major responsibility for rearing children, including their sons, it is their privilege with whatever assistance they can get from their spouses, to equip their sons fully for effective family living. In turn, it would enhance the race and the American society.

Conclusions.

An attempt has been made to examine the influence of age, sex, education, occupation, and income on authority, cooperative, and expressive family relations in a black Atlanta neighborhood, known here as Golden Towers. Several conclusions are suggested. First, this black middle-class neighborhood supports the finding that matriarchy characterizes some black families (Frazier, 1939; Hippler,

1974; Moynihan, 1967; and Powdermaker, 1962) and disagrees with the thesis that black matriarchy must be rejected as an insignificant family type (Cromwell and Cromwell, 1978 and Staples, 1977). Second, this study shows that matriarchal, patriarchal, and equalitarian family structures may be found in the black community. Third, the findings suggest elements that relate to each authority pattern. Fourth, a related finding is that the men in matriarchal households possess a relatively high degree of personal autonomy; hence, female control is not synonymous with control of spouse, although this may indeed occur. Fifth, several indices to matriarchy were found, including the extent of women's satisfaction with this type of family structure. It is by necessity rather than by preference that they make and implement most of the household decisions. Utilizing socioeconomic factors, it was shown that women who controlled decision making had more education and more prestigious occupations, but earned less money than their husbands. The economic role of husbands, therefore, did not support the finding in Hunter's Point that the men were often absent from the household and unsuited to steady employment (Hippler, 1974) and in Syracuse that men experienced a high rate of unemployment (Willie, 1976).

The sixth finding is that in the patriarchal households, the men make a majority of the decisions against their spouses' desires, but the women implement some of them and are responsible for household tasks. Seventh, the relatively high achievement of men is significantly related to patriarchy, and there are no men in those households with only elementary schooling. The eighth finding is that the men hold more prestigious jobs than their wives and usually earn more money.

Ninth, equalitarianism, the third type of family structure, is the most satisfying in the marriage complex and is related to socioeconomic factors. The women have achieved more education than their spouses, but 75 percent of the men had at least some college training. The women had more prestigious occupations, but less income than their husbands.

The tenth finding is that the elements related to the patterns of decision making in the black family suggest several implications. One is that a high level of education is an essential element to making a significant contribution to the family decision-making process in each family type. Furthermore, prestigious occupations are another key to the men's participation in either a patriarchal or equalitarian household, while income is basic in each type of household. To prevent matriarchy, income must be coupled with a relatively high level of education. It is also suggested here that a benign male socialization process, that is, inadequate training in decisiveness, good reasoning ability, and mechanical skills may lead to male ineffectiveness in the family decision-making process. Moreover, the extent to which skills learned during childhood and adulthood reach maturity is likely to be influenced by the wife's childhood socialization in attitudes toward black men and effective decision making.

The eleventh finding is that the men cooperate in the performance of house-related tasks; hence, this study does not support the finding in Newtown and Pulpwood Counties that a rigid division of labor occurs between spouses (Martin and Martin, 1978). Twelve, socio-economic factors are related to men's performance of household tasks. The highest percentage who perform household chores has either a college degree or college schooling, a blue collar occupation, and a $10,000 - $13,999 annual income. Additionally, the husbands of housewives do fewer house-related tasks than men whose wives work; and they are an occupationally heterogeneous group.

Thirteen, it was found that couples participate in expressive relations; nevertheless, it appears that only a minority of them experience a strong emotional bond. Hence, the women in Golden Towers do not completely support Bernard's (1966) finding that black women suffer less in the area of companionship and love than income and understanding. Although the women desire warmth and love, a finding supported by Scanzoni (1971), I did not find that they were alienated from their spouses (Staples, 1979) or denigrated male sexuality as found in Hunter's point (Hippler, 1974). Furthermore, several reasons explain the weak emotional link among some black spouses; men may lack sufficient income to support their family (a finding supported by Scanzoni, 1971) and the men engage in extramarital sex (a finding supported by Holloman and Lewis, 1978). Moreover, sometimes couples lack a strong emotional link because only one spouse assumes major responsibility for running the house; the spouses emphasize material things instead of personal relations in the childrearing process; and spouses are unequally interested in church participation and each other's friends. In addition, they experience inequality in education, occupation, and income. Finally, the ability and willing-ness to receive and give love to close kin and the personality type of husbands are likely to influence the quality of the marital bond.

In conclusion, the findings of this study seem to suggest that sex, education, occupation, income, and childhood and adulthood socialization are major determinants of spousal interaction and that black middle-class couples are both similar and different from lower- and working-class couples.

CHAPTER NINE

PARENTS AND CHILDREN,
STEPPARENTS AND STEPCHILDREN,
SIBLINGS AND GRANDPARENTS AND GRANDCHILDREN

Similar to husband and wife behavior, studies of parent and child relations have focused primarily on low-income and working class communities. In this chapter, I shall use the same types of relations found in these communities to analyze family relations in Golden Towers, a black middle class community. The main focus is the influence of age, sex, education, occupation, and income on parent and child, stepparent and stepchild, sibling, and grandparent and grandchild authority, cooperative, and affective relations.

The interaction of black parents and children has been seen as child disciplining, the province of mothers.[1] On St. Helena Island[2] and in Jamaica,[3] Carriacou,[4] and Hunter's Point, a San Francisco ghetto,[5] the women utilize corporal punishment to discipline their children. Moreover, in Newtown County, Missouri and Pulpwood County, Florida, working class neighborhoods, some black aged family members believe that "children should be seen but not heard."[6] The American black middle class children, however, are "generally subjected to strict disciplining, but are not treated with harshness, which is often found in the case of children in lower class families."[7]

Parent and child interaction has also been seen as cooperative behavior. In the Midwestern city of Jackson Harbor, adult blacks are primarily responsible for training and supervising children's performance of household tasks,[8] and when girls in Hunter's Point reach seven or eight years of age, they help their mothers with household tasks.[9]

Another area of parent and child interaction concerns expressive relations. Parents, for example, establish goals for them, which include "What white children have had and continue to have" and

113

values.[10] For example, in a black lower working class neighborhood, parental values for their children include strictness, responsibility, wise use of time, involvement in decision making, parental love, and goal achievement,[11] and the aged family members in Newtown County and Pulpwood County desire their young relatives to get a "good" education and learn the necessity of hard work.[12] Moreover, in Jackson Harbor, "the bond between mothers and their children is exceedingly strong and the majority of mothers in the Flats raise their own children"[13] while the emotional link between fathers and their children is determined by whether the father acknowledges or denies paternity.[14] On the other hand, in Holmes County, Mississippi, both parents "Feel an obligation to provide babies with physical affection, while contingent responsibility for the protection, care, instruction, and discipline of all children is diffused among related adults and indeed all adults."[15] Furthermore, in Hunter's Point infants are desired, mothers and other females love, fondle, touch and, play with them continually. However, around the first year of age, when the mother is irritated, has a visitor, or is watching one of her favorite television shows, the child receives harsh comments and gets locked out of the house; moreover, many of the child's complaints go unnoticed.[16] It has also been found that grandmothers often take care of young children while their mothers go to work;[17] besides, the black men in Spout Spring "give a great deal of time to their children."[18] Similarly, when the Andros Island father "is at home, he plays with the children."[19] According to Otterbein,[20] a stepfather's relationship with his stepchildren on the Andros Islands "Will probably be like that with his own children." Nevertheless, according to Firth,[21] Young and Willmott,[22] Adams,[23] Shimkin et al.[24] and Holloman and Lewis,[25] the mother and child bond is the strongest in the parent and child behavior complex.

When it comes to sibling relations, the need for research on sibling socialization has been emphasized.[26] However, it has been found that sibling relations are strong enough to be second only to the parent and child bond in the black family behavior complex.[27] Similarly, a strong bond also exists between grandparents and their grandchildren; in fact, privileged familiarity characterizes their relations.[28]

Parents and Children.

Disciplining. This discussion about the parents in Golden Towers and their ninety-four children (forty sons and fifty-four daughters) includes thirty-five families; six households were childless. As can be seen from Table 1, a high percentage (48.8) of all children were either only children or they had only one sibling. The next highest percentage (29.2) of the children were either one of three or four children, and the average number of children was approximately 2.7 per family. Of course, when the entire neighborhood was considered, the average number of children per household was approximately 2.3.

TABLE 1

Number of Children Born to Parents
by Number of Golden Towers Households
in Each Category

Number of Children Born	Households in Each Category	
	No.	Percent
Zero	6	14.6
One	10	24.4
Two	10	24.4
Three	6	14.6
Four	6	14.6
Seven	2	4.9
Eight	1	2.4
Total	41	99.9

Number of classes for which data on children born to parents by number of households in each category were secured.

The women in Golden Towers assumed the major responsibility for disciplining their children. The majority of the men left disciplining to them, because it was the tradition in one of the two parents' families, if not both, for mothers to administer punishment to daughters. According to the female respondents, this means that they were disciplined more than sons, which led to a somewhat benign male socialization process; hence, they were not taught as often as girls to be warm, loving, aggressive, successful, efficient, and decisive.

Although women assumed greater responsibility for control of their children, the men were more effective disciplinarians. The children adhered to their father's request quicker, for they were not as accustomed to his reprimands as they were to those given by their mother. Another reason why the men were more effective disciplinarians was that they spoke only a few words while women sometimes

115

"preached" on the issue; therefore, the men's brief discussion was either better understood or taken more seriously. Moreover, the women said that the voice tones of fathers were more convincing to children; the women's voices were quick, high, and sometimes sharp while fathers' voices, although higher than normal, were low and positive. Nevertheless, when taken together, the mothers' more detailed pattern and the fathers' more streamlined approach to child disciplining complemented each other and formed a coordinate system by which they were able to manage their children and prevent rigid control.

The Golden Towers parents utilized several disciplining techniques, including self-disciplining. It allowed the parents and children to decide their action. Confinement was another disciplining pattern; children were confined to their rooms, closets, and corners. Moreover, parent and child conferences were utilized to discipline children. A mother who utilized them explained to their daughter that they were hurt by her disobedience and both parents tried to develop in her a sense of obligation to them and their trust in her.

Children were also disciplined by denying them privileges. Parents denied them the opportunity to watch television, attend parties, go outside to play, stay up past their bedtime, use the telephone, entertain and visit friends, spend the night away from home, eat candy, and play with toys; but the most frequently denied privileges were watching television, going to events, and playing outside the house.

Threats of punishment were another method used to discipline children. A mother who failed to carry out her threats believed that spanking was cruel, but now she wishes that she had used corporal punishment. Nevertheless, approximately three-fourths (twenty-nine) of the families utilized it to discipline their children. Of this number, five applied it often and twenty-four parents used it occasionally; the parents of at least one son and one daughter applied corporal punishment equally to them. This finding indicates that sex of the children did not influence frequency of corporal punishment. The women used their hands, switches, rulers, brushes, shoes, newspapers, and their husband's belts to administer corporal punishment; all equipment was applied to children's bottoms, hands, and legs. Furthermore, at least one Golden Towers mother supplemented whipping with pinching the fattest parts of her children's bodies.

To more fully understand corporal punishment, I crosstabulated it with age. As noted in Table 2, women in all age categories utilized it, but the highest percentage was between thirty and forty nine years old. Table 2 also demonstrates that women on all educational levels employed corporal punishment; however, the highest percentage had college training. Moreover, women who had achieved the highest and lowest level of education comprised the lowest percentage that had utilized corporal punishment; conversely, those mothers who were at the middle range of educational achievement, college and masters degrees, had used it most frequently. It was also found, as noted in Table 3, that women on all occupational levels, service work excepted, utilized corporal punishment, but professional women and housewives employed corporal punishment more often than others. It was likely that the professional women used corporal punishment more often than most other women because they realized the full benefits of disciplining while the housewives not only realized its benefits, but they also had more time to devote to disciplining. Since the income data were incomplete, it was only possible to make a partial interpretation of its relationship to disciplining. Perhaps the most significant finding, as shown in Table 4, is that the women in the middle income range ($10,000-$13,999) were the most frequent users of corporal punishment.

Disciplining in this neighborhood was also developmental. Thus, varied techniques were employed to correct children who continually committed the same wrong act: when the child was admonished the first time for either committing or failing to commit a specific pattern of behavior, he was restricted to a certain part of the house, prevented from watching television, or going outside and experienced parental threats, change of voice, and admonishings; the second or third time that the child was reprimanded for the same act, one or more of the above punishments was utilized more extensively, or the child received corporal punishment. On the other hand, when a child committed a "serious act," such as lying, he was usually subjected to physical punishment.

Developmental disciplining was not only manifested in regard to a single type of behavior, but it also spanned one's childhood. In one household, for example, when the children were babies and bit their mother, while nursing, she said, "No, no" and tapped them lightly or stopped feeding them. Once they became toddlers, she said "No, no" a little louder and tapped their hands for misconduct. As they grew older, she spanked and whipped them, but when they reached the fifth grade, corporal punishment was replaced with confinement, followed by conferences. This developmental pattern,

117

TABLE 2

Corporal Punishment by Age and Education of Mother

Type of Punishment	Age	Doctoral No.	%	Master No.	%	College No.	%	High School No.	%	Elem. School No.	%	Total No.	%
Corporal	30–39	2	17.0	4	33.0	6	50.0	0	0.0	0	0.0	12	40.0
	40–49	0	0.0	2	29.0	5	71.0	0	0.0	0	0.0	7	23.0
	50–59	0	0.0	2	33.0	3	50.0	1	17.0	0	0.0	6	20.0
	60–69	0	0.0	0	0.0	2	50.0	1	25.0	1	25.0	4	13.0
	70–	0	0.0	0	0.0	0	0.0	0	0.0	1	100.0	1	3.0
	Total	2	7.0	8	27.0	16	53.0	2	7.0	2	7.0	30	99.0

TABLE 3

Corporal Punishment by Age and Occupation of Mother

Type of Punishment	Age	Professional No.	%	White Collar No.	%	Blue Collar No.	%	Service Worker No.	%	House Wife No.	%	Total No.	%
Corporal	30–39	10	83.0	1	8.0	0	0.0	0	0.0	1	8.0	12	40.0
	40–49	3	43.0	1	14.0	0	0.0	1	14.0	2	29.0	7	23.0
	50–59	3	50.0	2	33.0	0	0.0	0	0.0	1	17.0	6	20.0
	60–69	0	0.0	1	25.0	0	0.0	1	25.0	2	50.0	4	13.0
	70–	0	0.0	0	0.0	0	0.0	0	0.0	1	100.0	1	3.0
	Total	16	53.0	5	17.0	0	0.0	2	7.0	7	23.0	30	99.0

TABLE 4

Corporal Punishment by Age and Income of Mother

Type of Punishment	Age	2,000–5,999 No.	%	6,000–9,999 No.	%	10,000–13,999 No.	%	22,000–25,999 No.	%	Total No.	%
Corporal	30–39	1	14.0	1	14.0	4	57.0	1	14.0	7	44.0
	40–49	0	0.0	1	25.0	3	75.0	0	0.0	4	25.0
	50–59	3	60.0	1	20.0	1	20.0	0	0.0	5	31.0
	60–69	0	0.0	0	0.0	0	0.0	0	0.0	0	0.0
	70–	0	0.0	0	0.0	0	0.0	0	0.0	0	0.0
	Total	4	25.0	3	19.0	8	50.0	1	6.0	16	100.0

during one's childhood, was not as rigid in actual practice as presented here. Moreover, sometimes the disciplining pattern associated with each childhood stage merely dominated and was accompanied by other techniques and in homes where there were two or more children, several patterns of disciplining operated simultaneously.

Cooperative Behavior.

Cooperation is another type of parent and child behavior in Golden Towers. They cooperated in making decisions for the household; for example, children suggested colors of items purchased, including the interior of their new cars. Moreover, parents and children decided the family vacation sites and the children's curfew and discussed their requests to spend the night with their friends, which often resulted in compromises.

Mothers and their children, especially girls, also cooperated in the performance of household chores. There were some girls who performed tasks on an equal basis with their mothers while others performed only a few chores. The variation was a consequence of different interests in cooking, cleaning, and doing laundry. Moreover, without regard for sex, the children, ten years old or younger, helped with all household chores. Of course, some mothers found it easier to do the household tasks than to keep repeating the same assignment, without satisfactory response, to their children.

Affective Behavior.

Affective parent and child relations were conceptualized as parental goals and values for their children, frequent and satisfying communication and companionship, and the resolution of parent and child interaction. Some of the goals parents had for their children were courtesy to all people, selection of a spouse with high moral, economic, and educational characteristics, and achievement of high morals, appropriate social etiquette, and a college education. Moreover, in this order, parents taught their children such values as honesty and truthfulness, respect for elders and self respect, obedience to parents, disciplined minds, and good sleeping habits, and development of a sympathetic nature and good decision making skills. Parents believed that achievement of these goals and values would enable their children to experience a useful and happy life, strong marital relations, and enable their sons to become the economic leaders in their households.

119

Terms of address, including the ones parents employed to address their children, were another type of parent and child affective behavior. As indicated in Table 5, they employed four term categories to address their sons and seven term categories to address their daughters. Since almost twice as many term categories were employed to address girls, the sex of children was significantly. related to number of terms of address employed. Another difference was that fathers employed nicknames for their daughters less often than their mothers.

The children also used a variety of terms to address their parents, but sex of the children is significantly related to the number of term categories employed to address fathers (see Table 6); hence, the girls employed five term categories while the boys utilized three term categories to address their fathers. Perhaps it should be related that the terms Daddy or uncle and first or last name and Mr. and first name were employed by stepchildren. Of course, as noted in Table 7, more terms were employed by both sexes to address their mothers than to address their fathers. This seems to indicate that a stronger emotional relationship exists between the women and their children than between the fathers and their children. Besides number of term categories, the types both sexes employed to address their mothers also support this proposition; the children's terms for them conveyed more warmth and informality than those employed to address their fathers.

TABLE 5

Parents' Terms of Address for Their Children
in Golden Towers

Terms of address	Father's Terms of Address for Sons	Mother's Terms of Address for Sons	Father's Terms of Address for Daughters	Mother's Terms of Address for Daughters
First Name	10	8	15	13
First Name & an Endearing Term	1	2	2	1
First Name & a Nickname	0	0	2	2
Middle Name	0	0	0	0
Endearing Name	0	0	2	1
Nickname	6	6	3	6
Nickname & First Name	0	1	0	1
Total	17	17	24	24

Number of households = 30

120

TABLE 6

Children's Terms of Address for Their Fathers
in Golden Towers

Terms of Address	Sons' Terms of Address for Their Fathers	Daughters' Terms of Address for Their Fathers
Daddy	16	21
My Daddy & Daddy	1	1
Da Da	0	1
Daddy Or Uncle & First Name or Last Name	1	1
Mr. & First Name	0	1
Nickname	1	1
Total	19	26

Number of households = 30

TABLE 7

Children's Terms of Address for Their Mothers
in Golden Towers

Terms of Address	Sons' Terms of Address for Their Mothers	Daughters' Terms of Address for Their Mothers
Mama	10	12
Mother	2	6
Mama-Mother	2	0
Mama & First Name	1	0
Mama-Mother Dear	1	1
Mama Dear	1	0
Mommy	1	5
Endearing Term	1	1
Nickname & Mama	0	1
Total	19	26

Number of households = 30

121

Conversation was another type of affective behavior shared by parents, especially mothers, and their children. They talked about a variety of subjects, including God. When one woman's daughter, for example, was five and a half years old, she asked, "Mama, who is God?" The mother replied, "He makes little girls and good Daddys." Five minutes later the child went outdoors and came back in the house and told her mother that the wind had kissed her cheeks, and that she knew it was God. When her daughter grew older, they often discussed sex. During those discussions, the mother explained to her daughter that a boy's erection was normal, and that one day, after marriage, he was likely to become a father; hence, it was no reason for her to misbehave. Moreover, she told her that if she found sex overpowering, that she should let her know. This mother also taught her daughter that, if she could not walk with the best, it was better to walk alone. To help her walk with the best, starting at age twelve, she invited her daughter's friends to seated luncheons in their home, taught her to smile, laugh, and engage in stimulating conversation, and sponsored theater parties. There were five girls in the group from prominent Atlanta families and each made a vow to this woman and to themselves to remain a virgin until their wedding day. Her own daughter promised that if she were not a virgin on her wedding day, she would not wear a veil. According to this mother, on her wedding day, she wore a veil, and her husband told her, "Thank you for giving me a wonderful and beautiful wife."

In another case, a mother and her son talked a great deal about his problems in the Atlanta Student Orchestra. When he made a mistake playing the drums, the conductor reprimanded him, because he wanted a white student to take his place, his mother reported. To keep from getting expelled, the mother told her son to be present at all band rehearsals and, regardless of what the band director said to him, he must hold his peace and bite his lips until they bled. In the meantime, the son learned to play another instrument, moved to a new position in the band, and developed a friendship with the band director. All of this was necessary, she said, for "blacks must always outdo whites to hold their places." This supports the assessment of blacks' circumstances by a respondent in a study made by Kronus. He reported that to be on the same level with whites, middle class blacks must "continue to be just a little better."

The women also discussed with their daughters appropriate social behavior. A woman, for example, had spent a great deal of time teaching her daughter how to walk and how to sit with her right foot, crossed at the ankles, over her left foot.

Another mother taught her son how to extend courtesy to all "Colored Women." In still another case, a woman was grooming her son to respect womanhood by practicing on her and his sister. Hence, for his sister, he daily took her car out of the garage, warmed it up in the winter, treated her gently, and escorted her to parties. This young man was a much sought after escort, and the mothers seemed pleased to entrust their daughters to him.

Companionship was another type of parent and child expressive behavior. Fathers and their sons attended athletic events, went fishing, swimming, shopping for food, minibikes, and clothing, played ping-pong, checkers, baseball, tennis, pool, cards, badminton, and dominoes, and assembled and played with toys; moreover, they watched sports on television and did school work. On the other hand, unless there were no boys in the home, the men's activities with their daughters usually included only transporting them to social and religious events. However, parent and child behavior was not engaged in on a regular basis; instead, it occurred when the men were not too tired or busy. Consequently, the men did not spend enough time with their children. The women were also involved in activities with their children, such as playing games, cooking, shopping, and attending church, movies, and cultural events, but they also were often too tired to play with their children. Thus, a majority of the women also failed to spend enough time playing with them; in fact, the men were more likely to play with their children than the women.

Gift giving was the next type of parent and child expressive behavior. Children received gifts from both parents on their birthdays and at Christmas. Parental gifts to children at Christmas were arranged high and wide around the Christmas trees and were a varied assortment of toys, dolls, stuffed animals, games, radios, record players, cameras, bicycles, minibikes, cars, books, records, tapes, filmstrips, telescopes, cosmetics, jewelry, and clothing. This list suggests that need and emphasis on recreation, education, and glamour help explain why parents gave children gifts and indicate that girls received more gifts than boys.

The manifestation of warmth also characterized expressive parent and child relations. The men, for example, enjoyed a congenial relationship with their children. A case in point was a father who enjoyed a "warm and respectful" relationship with his son; in another case, a father was a great friend of his daughter," and a girl who looked very much like her father was his "heart." Mothers and their children also expressed affection; hence, a nine year old son kissed his mother when he awakened and left for school, and a seven year old son stayed close to his mother and helped her serve meals. Moreover, several women were observed touching and talking with their children and sharing fun; besides, one set of parents helped entertain their daughter's boyfriend.

Nevertheless, affective relations did not circumvent conflict. It was often customary for parents, especially mothers, to make a "spirited effort" to maintain friendly relations with their children of both sexes. For example, as soon as problems developed between a mother and her two children that threatened to alienate them, she vigorously pursued them by keeping communication intact and during disagreements, she attempted to let them know that she understood their position while trying to make her point.

Emotional Bond.

The parent and child behavior complex revealed the closeness of parents and their children. Closeness was conceptualized as a pal or relaxed type of relationship. On this basis, twenty-seven children in Golden Towers were closer to their fathers than to their mothers and twenty-six of them were closer to their mothers than to their fathers; hence, there was no significant relationship between sex of parent and closeness to children. On the other hand, the analysis of pal relationships, by sex of children, showed interesting patterns; for instance, more daughters were closer to their fathers than to their mothers while some sons were closer to their mothers than to their fathers. It is likely that these patterns existed because parents and children of the opposite sex were not in competition with each other as often as parents and children of the same sex, and parents, especially fathers, did not discipline children of the opposite sex as often as they corrected children of their own sex.

Although there was a strong cross sex parent and child bond, mothers had a special relationship with all their children. Thus, both sexes depended on their mother to satisfy their needs and discuss their personal matters. The children depended more on their mothers than their fathers because they often found it easier to talk with them, mothers and daughters had things to talk about that fathers and daughters did not discuss, and the women spent more time with their children and took better care of their basic needs than fathers. As a result, if the nature of relations between fathers and mothers and their children is to be fully understood, satisfaction of the children's needs and conversations about their personal matters are not to be evaluated jointly with a relaxed parent and child relationship. Moreover, the closeness, in different areas of living, afforded children meaningful contact with parents. This analysis also revealed that a child is often close to a different parent at different ages. For example, at one time, a son was closer to his mother than to his father, but later he "straddled the fence," thereby making it difficult to determine which parent he liked better. Eventually he became closer to his father than to his mother. Consequently, from birth to adolescence, parent and child relations in Golden Towers were often in flux.

Stepparent and Stepchild Relations.

Authority, Cooperative and Affective Relations. There were five stepparents, three men and two women, who lived in five of the Golden Towers homes. The stepchild in one of the homes was grown, but unmarried children lived in the remainder of the homes. These four cases were studied to determine the influence of age and sex on their relations. It was found that stepfathers disciplined their stepchildren, especially their stepsons, but without the use of corporal punishment; for instance, one stepfather never punished his stepdaughter, but he disciplined his older stepson (the middle child) by taking privileges from him, including riding his minibike. On the other hand, when his younger stepson misbehaved, he sent him to bed or denied him privileges. Stepfathers and their stepchildren, especially stepsons, also cooperated in the performance of men's work, including mowing the lawn and repairing minibikes. Another finding is that stepfathers and their stepchildren shared affective behavior. Stepfathers were concerned about their stepchildren's education and talked in terms of the educational goals they and the children's mother had for them. Moreover, the stepfather and stepchild relations were respectful, relaxed, and congenial; hence, stepchildren, especially stepdaughters, attempted to get their stepfathers to grant permission, denied them by their mothers, asked their opinions, and called them "uncle" or "daddy" plus their first names. Thus, the stepfather and stepchild relationship closely resembled father and child interaction.

Unlike stepfather and stepchild behavior, the Golden Towers stepmother and stepchild relationships were varied. Stepmothers, like stepfathers, usually disciplined their stepchildren, but without using corporal punishment. Stepmothers and their stepchildren also cooperated with each other; hence, stepmothers taught their stepdaughters how to clean, cook, and serve meals, and in turn, the women satisfied the routine needs of their stepchildren. Stepmothers and their stepchildren also shared affective behavior. In one home, relations were somewhat tense while, in other homes, congenial interaction was experienced, but younger stepchildren and those of the opposite sex experienced more warmth with stepmothers than stepchildren over twelve years old and of the same sex as the stepmother. One stepmother, for example, maintained a warm relationship with her eleven year old stepson, refereed differences between him and his father, purchased his clothing, and accompanied him on important occasions. Furthermore, stepsons often told their problems to stepmothers, before their fathers found out about them, and stepchildren of both sexes usually called their stepmothers by their first names (Mother was sometimes used by younger children).

Siblings.

Authority, Cooperative and Affective Relations. This section of the chapter examines the influence of age and sex on sibling relations and the nature of the socialization process. The siblings engaged in varied behavior, including authority relations. Older children, especially girls, supervised younger children by admonishing them or attempting to apply corporal punishment; for example, an older female sibling requested her younger brother to put on certain garments and chased him with their father's belt until he returned to his room. Siblings also cooperated with each other; they mowed and raked the lawns, made beds, and decorated their rooms together. Moreover, there were a few siblings who complimented each other on their appearance, achievement, and talent, and discussed their friends, problems, television shows, games, and new dances. Besides, siblings showed kindness to one another. To appreciate its extent, consider the following case. When the mother of four children threatened to apply corporal punishment, the remainder of the siblings attempted to explain why their brother or sister was not guilty. When the mother established guilt, they tried to convince her that their sibling should not be punished.

Companionship was another type of affective behavior and was most vivid between siblings of the same sex. Sisters shopped, swam, attended Sunday School, church, ceremonies, parades, and movies, helped younger female siblings to understand them, listened to records, and talked. In other cases, brothers played basketball, rode minibikes, raked the lawn, and assembled motor cars. For many years, the older siblings had socialized their younger siblings, especially same sex siblings, but there were at least two siblings of the same sex who experienced sibling rivalry as a result of school competition.

There were also cross-sex siblings who experienced antagonism. Thus, in five households, tension existed between male and female children; in one family, an older brother experienced a warm relationship with his baby brother, but he was often in conflict with his older sister. Their mother prevented them from fighting and tried to teach them to respect and love each other. In another household, a male and female sibling usually remained in their separate rooms, and in a similar case, each sibling remained in his room and watched his favorite television shows; an exception occurred when the sister visited her brother's room. In a fourth household, a brother played well with his younger sister, but he did not like for his older sisters to dominate him, and in a fifth household, a brother disliked being disciplined by his sister. The male siblings ranged in age from eight to thirteen years and were younger than their sisters. According to their parents, cross sex tension existed because the young male siblings disliked being dominated by their sisters. This finding was supported by cross sex siblings who experienced congenial relations. For example, a fifteen year old boy and his twelve year old sister enjoyed making desserts and accompanying their father on household errands. Of course, antagonism did not characterize all older female and younger male sibling relations; thus, a younger brother and his older sister shared a congenial relationship.

Although sibling behavior was complex, it is clear that siblings interacted with each other and that the dominant trend, prior to the teens, was that siblings near each other's age were closer to one another than to their older siblings; and when they reached their teens, the relationship was closer between siblings of the same sex than between cross sex siblings.

Grandparent and Grandchild Relations.

Authority, Cooperative and Affective Relations. Grandparents also helped to make up the Golden Towers household. A grandmother lived in seven households; five were paternal and two were maternal grandmothers. There were also two sets of grandparents with homes in which a son and his wife and child lived. In another household, two grandchildren lived with their grandparents; in still another, grandparents, their children, and their children's children lived together, and a divorced daughter and her unmarried daughter lived in the home of the widowed grandmother; consequently, grandparents

127

and grandchildren shared twelve of the forty-one households.

The influence of age and sex on grandparent and grandchild authority, cooperative, and afffective relations is now considered. Similar to siblings, grandparents and their grandchildren engaged in varied types of interaction, including disciplining. However, grandfathers rarely disciplined their grandchildren, especially granddaughters. On the other hand, grandfathers and their children cooperated with each other; it was most vivid when they assembled a new toy. Moreover, affective behavior was the strongest relationship between grandfathers and their grandchildren. Grandfathers showed immense interest in their accomplishments, gave them gifts, and talked, laughed, and played with them; for example, one grandfather played baseball with his grandsons. The grandchildren's grandfathers also held them, especially granddaughters on their knees.

On the other hand, grandmothers interacted more than grandfathers with their grandchildren. They disciplined their grandchildren and assigned and helped them perform household chores. The grandchildren, however, did not perform duties required by their grandmothers as quickly as when their parents gave them chores. And the grandmothers and their grandchildren shared a strong affective relationship. The grandmothers talked, laughed, and played with them, and encouraged them to be smart in school. The relationship between grandparents and their grandchildren was more relaxed and playful than existed between children and their parents and, thus, supports the theory that grandchildren and grandparents enjoy a congenial relationship; however, since grandmothers disciplined and controlled their children more than fathers, in Golden Towers, their relations were less congenial than grandfather and grandchild behavior.

Conclusions.

This chapter has examined the influence of age, sex, education, occupation, and income on family relations, including parent and child interaction. It was concluded that the women assumed more responsibility than the men for disciplining their children, because this was the traditional pattern in their own families, a finding supported by Young (1970), Hippler (1974), and Willie (1976). Another conclusion was that failure of the men to constantly discipline their children, especially their sons, resulted in the girls receiving more training than the boys in the development of warmth, the ability to love, constructive aggression, success, efficiency, and decisiveness. It was next concluded that although the women assumed greater

128

responsibility for control of their children, the men were more effective disciplinarians, and the detailed approach of the mother and the streamlined approach of the father resulted in effective disciplining. It was also concluded that the multidisciplinary techniques, including self-disciplining, confinement, establishment of the child's sense of obligation to parents and their trust in the child, denial of privileges, parent and child conferences, threats, corporal punishment, employed to control children in Golden Towers did not coincide with the multidisciplinary techniques of negative comments, locking children outdoors and ignoring some of their demands, found by Hippler (1974) in Hunter's Point. Of course, this study supports the finding that black families employ corporal punishment found by Woofter (1930), Smith (1962), Hippler (1974), and Clarke (1975). Moreover, it was found that the sex of children in Golden Towers was not related to frequency of corporal punishment. The Golden Towers disciplinary pattern also supports Frazier's (1957) finding that black middle class children are subject to strict, but not harsh disciplining. It was further concluded that women in all age, educational, occupational, and income (one excepted) categories had utilized corporal punishment, but the most frequent users were women between thirty and forty-nine years of age, who had achieved college training, a professional occupation, and the middle income range, $10,000 - $13,999. Three related findings were that women who had achieved the highest and lowest education tended to refrain from using corporal punishment; for women on the lower end of the socioeconomic scale, income was more significant than education and occupation for determining use of corporal punishment; and for those on the middle point on the scale, the use of corporal punishment was associated with education, occupation, and income. Moreover, disciplining was found to be developmental and was experienced by both sexes.

Another conclusion was that cooperation was characteristic of parent and child interaction, a finding supported by Stack (1974) and Hippler (1974). They cooperated in making decisions about the household and children's curfew; hence, this study does not support Martin and Martin's (1978) finding that "children should be seen and not heard." The women and their children also cooperated in the performance of household tasks, and for children ten years old and younger, sex was not a significant determinant of children's participation in the performance of household tasks.

It was further concluded that this study supports the finding that affective behavior is another type of parent and child interaction (Scanzoni, 1971; Stack, 1974; Martin and Martin, 1978; Bartz and

Levine, 1978). It included parental goals for their children; parents planned the eduction, occupation, income, moral, manners, and personal qualities they would like to see demonstrated. However, for males, more emphasis was placed on achievement of goals while morals, manners, and personal qualities were the main concern for females. Another type of affective behavior was parents' terms of address for their children. The sex of the child, however, is significantly related to the number of terms of address employed; four terms were used to address sons and seven were employed to address girls. it was likely that the difference in number of terms suggests greater friendliness between girls and their parents than between boys and their parents. The children's terms of address for their parents also conveyed warmth; however, the terms employed to address mothers conveyed more warmth and informality than those employed to address fathers. Moreover, the girls employed four terms to address their fathers while the boys employed three terms to address them, and both sexes employed more terms to address their mother than their father. Again, this is likely to indicate greater familiarity and warmth between children and their mothers than between fathers and their children. Conversation about God, sex, appropriate treatment of black women, and social behavior was another type of affective behavior. Most of the talk, however, took place between mothers and their children.

Another conclusion was that parents and their children engaged in companionate behavior, but it was inadequate because parents were too busy and too tired to spend enough time with them; moreover, fathers were more likely to play with children than their mothers. As if to compensate for this void in their children's lives, another type of affective behavior was gift giving. Gifts were given to both sexes on their birthday and at Christmas and constituted a major behavior complex in this neighborhood; however, it appeared that girls received more gifts than boys at Christmas. The gift giving complex, at least temporarily, appeared to enhance the children's excitement for their parents.

It was also found that an emotional bond characterized parent and child interaction. Hence, the sex proposition influenced parent and child emotional relations; when a pal type relationship was considered, the cross sex parent and child emotional bond was stronger than the father and child relationship. Besides, during the growing up period, a child was often closer to a different parent at different stages.

130

It was further concluded that this study supports the finding that parent and child interaction, especially mothers and their children, is the strongest in the family complex (Firth, 1956; Young and Willmott, 1957; Adams, 1968; Shimkin, 1978). Moreover, it was concluded that conflict arose between parents and their children of both sexes, but mothers assumed major responsibility for resolving their problems.

This analysis of stepparent and stepchild behavior also revealed the significance of age and sex on their behavior. It was concluded that a stronger stepfather and stepchild bond than stepmother and stepchild bond existed; however, stepfathers and their stepdaughters experienced the most congenial relations, and a stronger emotional bond existed between stepparents and stepchildren under twelve years of age than with older stepchildren.

It was concluded concerning sibling interaction that younger siblings near each other's age, regardless of sex, seemed closer to one another than to same sex older siblings, and siblings of the same sex, during their teen years, were closer to their same sex siblings than cross sex siblings. Furthermore, older male and younger female siblings were more congenial than younger male and older female siblings, a consequence of male siblings' resentment of their sister's domination. Another finding was that this study supports Shimkin's (1978) finding that sibling relations were strong enough to be second only to the mother and child bond. On the other hand, sibling rivalry was found to characterize relations between one set of siblings and antagonism existed between a few cross sex siblings. Moreover, authority relations characterized sibling interaction; age determined which sibling had more authority, and older siblings socialized younger siblings of both sexes. Consequently, sibling behavior in Golden Towers supports Irish's (1964) sibling socialization principle.

Finally, sex and age were significant determinants of grandparent and grandchild interaction. Since they had a semi-equalitarian relationship, Radcliffe-Brown's (1950) principle of privileged familiarity was also supported. Besides, sex of grandparents influenced family relations; hence, grandfathers and their grandchildren experienced more congenial relations than grandmothers and their grandchildren, because they disciplined less and assigned fewer chores.

This study, therefore, seems to support the hypothesis that age, sex, education, occupation, and income were major determinants of interaction in the Golden Towers family.

131

NOTES

1. Virginia Hayer Young. "Family and Childhood in A Southern Negro Community." AMERICAN ANTHROPOLOGIST 72:283.

2. T. J. Woofter. BLACK YEOMANRY. New York: Henry Holt & Co., 1930, p. 212.

3. Edith Clarke. MY MOTHER WHO FATHERED ME. London: George Allen and Unwin, 1957, pp. 100, 168.

4. M. G. Smith. KINSHIP AND COMMUNITY IN CARRIACOU. New Haven: Yale University Press, 1962, pp. 100, 119, 146).

5. Arthur E. Hippler. HUNTER'S POINT. New York: Basic Books, Inc., 1974, p. 28.

6. Elmer P. Martin and Joanne Mitchell Martin. THE BLACK EXTENDED FAMILY. Chicago: The University of Chicago Press, 1978, p. 51.

7. E. Franklin Frazier. THE NEGRO IN THE UNITED STATES. New York: The MacMillan Co., 1957. p. 330.

8. Carol B. Stack. ALL OUR KIN. New York: Harper & Row Publishers, 1974, p. 6.

9. Arthur E. Hippler. HUNTER'S POINT. op. cit., p. 28.

10. John H. Scanzoni. THE BLACK FAMILY IN MODERN SOCIETY. Boston: Allyn and Bacon, Inc., 1971, pp. 278, 293.

11. Karen W. Bartz and Elaine S. Levine. "Childrearing by Black Parents: A Description and Comparison of Anglo and Chicano Parents." JOURNAL OF MARRIAGE AND THE FAMILY, 1978, 4:717-718.

12. Elmer P. Martin and Joanne Mitchell Martin. THE BLACK EXTENDED FAMILY. Chicago: The University of Chicago Press, 1978, p. 52.

13. Carol B. Stack. ALL OUR KIN. New York: Harper & Row, Publishers, 1974, p. 48.

14. **Ibid.**, pp. 51-53.

15. Demitri B. Shimkin et al. "The Black Extended Family: A Basic Rural Institution and A Mechanism of Urban Adaptation. In THE EXTENDED FAMILY IN BLACK SOCIETIES. The Hague: Mouton Publishers, 1978, p. 72.

16. Arthur E. Hippler. HUNTER'S POINT. op. cit., pp. 22-25.

17. Charles V. Willie. A NEW LOOK AT BLACK FAMILIES. Bayside: General Hall Publishers, 1976, p. 161.

18. Peter Kunkel and Sara Sue Kennard. SPOUT SPRING. New York: Holt, Rinehart and Winston, Inc., 1971, p. 46.

19. Keith F. Otterbein. THE ANDROS ISLANDERS. Lawrence: University of Kansas Publishers, 1966, p. 118.

20. **Ibid.**, p. 123.

21. Raymond Firth. TWO STUDIES OF KINSHIP IN LONDON. London: Athlone Press, 1956, p. 63.

22. Michael Young and Peter Willmott. FAMILY AND KINSHIP IN EAST LONDON. London: Routledge and Kegan Paul, 1957, p. 157.

23. Bert N. Adams. KINSHIP IN AN URBAN SETTING. Chicago: Markham Publishers, 1968, p. 169.

24. Demitri B. Shimkin et al. THE BLACK EXTENDED FAMILY. Op. cit., pp. 249-250.

25. Regina E. Holloman and Fannie E. Lewis. "The Clan: Case Study of a Black Extended Family in Chicago." In Demitri B. Shimkin, et. al. THE EXTENDED FAMILY IN BLACK SOCIETIES, 1978, p. 226.

26. Donald P. Irish. "Sibling Interaction." SOCIAL FORCES 1964, 42: 279-288.

27. Demitri B. Shimkin et al. THE BLACK EXTENDED FAMILY, op. cit., pp. 70, 249.

28. A. R. Radcliffe-Brown and Daryll Forde. AFRICAN SYSTEMS OF KINSHIP AND MARRIAGE. New York: Oxford University Press, 1950, p. 29.

CHAPTER TEN

INTERPRETATIONS

This work is based on ten and one-half months of fieldwork (September, 1969 to July 1970), for my dissertation, using numerous methods of collecting data. The location of this study was a residential neighborhood in Atlanta composed of black households, most of which could be characterized as solid middle class by contemporary American standards. the neighborhood is called "Golden Towers" in this study since it symbolizes the goal of the good life for which almost all Americans seem to strive. The families in Golden Towers had not only reached the goal, but they are black. Most family and neighborhood studies of black Americans in the past have focused upon lower-class blacks in urban ghettos. Actually, very little is known from social research about middle-class blacks. The paucity of research in this area suggested that study of a neighborhood such as Golden Towers might help to fill a gap in research whose existence has tended to add to the stereotype of black Americans as poor, uneducated, struggling for survival and equipped with all of the pathologies deriving from urban poverty.

There is a general tendency in American society to assume that whites are by some standard middle class. That is, upon first contact, a white person is likely to be accorded the deference and respect that is normally accorded middle class persons. Unless there are rather obvious and detectable indications to the contrary; however, a black person is likely to be held to have a lower class life style. He is thereafter treated with the lack of deference and respect in the manner considered appropriate for dealing with persons of a low status. Since the benefit of the doubt is given to whites, but the reverse occurs with blacks, one would expect black families of comfortable means and good education to not only optimize material and behavior symbols of social rank to assure that their relative social worth is not misperceived, but to train their children in such a way that increases their chances of achieving and communicating

137

the ranking of their family of orientation. This is indeed what was found in the study of Golden Towers.

Although the black subsociety and neighborhood were the location of research, the unit of analysis was the household. Each household was seen as the central focus of social interaction for the residents of Golden Towers, an assumption amply verified by my field research. The question of location of social interaction arose from the assumption of a black ethnic sobsociety. Outside the household itself, where do black people in Golden Towers "plug into" the social world around them? By answering this question, it was hoped that the existence and relative strength of the black subsociety could be determined.

The results of my investigation suggest that the strongest ties were household and kin network (see PHYLON, XLII:369-380 for a discussion of kinship). In terms of the sheer volume of time, much social interaction in the real world took place largely outside the black subsociety in the dominant white society (see JOURNAL OF SOCIAL AND BEHAVIORAL SCIENCES 238:353-360 for a discussion of the status of Atlanta blacks in the workplace). Abrasive contacts, real and perceived insults, slights and restricted employment opportunites in this sphere of interaction fed again into the family interaction pattern, reinforcing the need for solidarity and intimacy in the household.

In the realm of voluntary association participation, it was found that interaction takes place almost exclusively with other black people, especially when interaction is informal. Churches in which Golden Towers families held membership were composed of all black congregations. They also helped to maintain the boundaries of the racial groups by focusing ethnical applications and group sentiment upon cases in which blacks are discriminated against, sometimes calling for social action of various kinds.

It is the neighborhood, also solidly black in residential composition in which social interaction is weakest. Interaction tended to be dyadic, tying two households together in telephoning and visiting patterns. Extensity of social contact was not the norm. Norms favoring mutual aid in times of family crisis did exist and became temporarily operative when appropriate. There was a neighborhood club which provided a potential or incipient basis for neighborhood interaction, but it remained in the background. In short, Golden Towers itself was not a locus of much social interaction. It was a neighborhood but not a community. The existence of a black ethnic subsociety was verified by interaction patterns within and extending from the households studied, but the residential neighborhood itself played a very small role in the subsociety, except as a symbol of the good life for aspiring blacks, as noted in the chapter on the household setting and its environs, and as a location for the most significant interaction in the population studied, that is, in the household itself.

BIBLIOGRAPHY

Adams, Bert N., KINSHIP IN AN URBAN SETTING. Chicago: Markham Publishing Company, 1968.

Adams, Samuel L. BLUEPRINTS FOR SEGREGATION: A SURVEY OF ATLANTA HOUSING. Atlanta: The City of Atlanta, 1967.

Allen Temple African Methodist Church, EXCERPT HISTORY. Atlanta: Allen Temple African Methodist Church, 1968.

Bacoate, Clarence. THE STORY OF ATLANTA UNIVERSITY. Princeton: Princeton University Press, 1969.

Bartz, Karen W. and Elaine S. Levine. "Childrearing by Black Parents: A Description and Comparison of Anglo and Chicano Parents." JOURNAL OF MARRIAGE AND THE FAMILY, 40, 1978, pp. 709-719.

Bernard, Jessie. MARRIAGE AND FAMILY AMONG NEGROES. Englewood Cliffs: prentice Hall, 1966.

Berry, Brian J. L. and Frank E. Horton. GEOGRAPHIC PRESPECTIVES ON URBAN SYSTEMS. Englewood Cliffs: Princeton Hall, Inc. 1970.

Berry, Brian J. L. et. al. CHICAGO: TRANSFORMATIONS OF AN URBAN SYSTEM. Cambridge: Ballinger Publishing Company, 1976.

Bossard, James and Eleanor S. Boll. RITUAL IN FAMILY LIVING. Philadelphia: University of Pennsylvania Press, 1950.

Brink, William and Louis Harris. THE NEGRO REVOLUTION. New York: Simon and Schuster, 1964.

Brittin, Helen C. and Dale W. Zinn. "Meat Buying Practices of Caucasians, Mexican Americans, and Negroes." JOURNAL OF THE AMERI-
CAN DIETETIC ASSOCIATION, 71, 1977, pp. 623-628.

Bullock, Henry A. THE TEXAS NEGRO FAMILY: THE STATUS
OF ITS SOCIOECONOMIC ORGANIZATION. Prairie View: Prairie
View College Press, 1941.

Chapman, Dennis. THE HOME AND SOCIAL STATUS. New York:
Grove Press, 1955.

City of Atlanta. LAND LOT BOOK 230, 249, 259. Atlanta: City
of Atlanta.

Clark, Johnnie L. "Planning, MARTA, and the City's Future Direction
- A Response." In THE FUTURE OF ATLANTA'S CENTRAL CITY,
Edwin N. Gorsuch and Dudley S. Hinds (eds.). Atlanta: Publishing
Services Division, College of Business Administration/Georgia State
University, 1977, pp. 46-51.

Clarke, Edith. MY MOTHER WHO FATHERED ME. London: George
Allen and Unwin, 1957.

Codere Helen. "A Genealogical Study of Kinship in the United States,"
PSYCHIATRY, 1955, XVIII, pp. 65-79.

Cromwell, Vickey L. and Ronald E. Cromwell. "Perceived Dominance
in Decision-Making and Conflict Resolution Among Anglo, Black
and Chicano Couples," JOURNAL OF MARRIAGE AND THE FAMILY,
1978, 40, 749-759.

Darden, Joe T. AFROAMERICANS IN PITTSBURGH. Lexington:
D. C. Heath and Company, 1973.

Drake, St. Clair and Horace R. Clayton. BLACK METROPOLIS,
Vol. II. New York: Harper and Row Publishers, 1945.

Dubois, W. E. B. SOME EFFECTS OF AMERICAN NEGROES FOR
THEIR BETTERMENT. Atlanta: Atlanta University Press, 1898.

Firth, Raymond. TWO STUDIES OF KINSHIP IN LONDON. London:
Athlone Press, 1956.

Frazier, E. Franklin. THE NEGRO FAMILY IN THE UNITED STATES. Chicago: The University of Chicago Press, 1939.

Frazier, E. Franklin. THE NEGRO IN THE UNITED STATES. New York: the Macmillan Company, 1957.

Frazier, E. Franklin. THE NEGRO CHURCH IN AMERICA. New York: Schecker Books, 1963.

Garrett, Franklin M. ATLANTA AND ITS ENVIRONS, Vol 1. New York: Lewis Historical Publishing Company, 1954.

Garrett, Franklin M. "Atlanta and Its Environs," THE ATLANTA HISTORICAL BULLETIN, XIV, 4 (December 1969).

Goffman, Irving. "Symbols of Class Status!" BRITISH JOURNAL OF SOCIOLOGY, II, 4 (December 1951).

Grier, George and Eunice Grier. EQUALITY AND BEYOND. Chicago: Quandrangle Books, 1966.

Grodzins, Morton. THE METROPOLITAN AREA AS A RACIAL PROBLEM. Pittsburgh: University of Pittsburgh Press, 1958.

Hartshone, Turman A. METROPOLIS IN GEORGIA: ATLANTA'S RISE AS A MAJOR TRANSACTION CENTER. Cambridge: Ballinger Publishing Co., 1976.

Hippler, Arthur E. HUNTER'S POINT. New York: Basic Books, Inc., 1974.

Holloman, Regina E. and Fannie E. Lewis. "The Clan: Case Study of a Black Extended Family in Chicago," In D. B. Shimkin et al. (eds.) THE EXTENDED FAMILY IN BLACK SOCIETIES. The Hague: Mouton Publishers, 1978, 201-238.

Irish, Donald P. "Sibling Interaction." SOCIAL FORCES. 42, 1964, pp. 279-288.

King, Charles E. "The Negro Maternal Family: A Product of an Economic and A Culture System." SOCIAL FORCES, 1945, 24 (October), 100-104.

Koh, Eunsook T. and Virginia Caples. "Nutrient Intake of Low-Income Black Families in Southwestern Mississippi." JOURNAL OF THE AMERICAN DIETETIC ASSOCIATION, 75, 1970, pp. 665-670.

Koh, Eunsook T. and Virginia Caples. "Frequency of Selection of Food Groups by Low-Income Families in Southwestern Mississippi. JOURNAL OF THE AMERICAN DIETETIC ASSOCIATION. 74, 1979, pp. 660-664.

Kronus, Sidney. THE BLACK MIDDLE CLASS. Columbus: Charles E. Merrill Publishing Company, 1971.

Kunkel, Peter and Sara Sue Kennard. SPOUT SPRING. New York: Holt, Rinehart and Winston, Inc., 1971.

MacIver, R. M. THE SOCIETY. Chicago: University of Chicago Press, 1970.

Martin, Elmer P. and Joanne Mitchell Martin. THE BLACK EXTENDED FAMILY. Chicago: The Univeristy of Chicago Press, 1978.

Mead, Margaret. "The Contemporary American Family as an Anthropologist Sees It." AMERICAN JOURNAL OF SOCIOLOGY, 53:453-459 (July 1947 - May 1948).

Mount Zion Second Baptist Church. CENTENNIAL BOOKLET, 1868--1968. Atlanta: Mount Zion Second Baptist Church, 1968.

Moynihan, Daniel P. "The Roots of the Problem," In Lee Rainwater and William L. Yancey (eds.) THE MOYNIHAN REPORT AND THE POLITICS OF CONTROVERSY. Cambridge: The M.I.T. Press, 1967.

Otterbein, Keith F. THE ANDROS ISLANDERS. Lawrence: University of Kansas Publishers, 1966.

Powdermaker, Hortense. COPPER TOWN: CHANGING AFRICA. New York: Harper & Row Publishers, 1962.

Radcliffe-Brown, A. R. and Daryll Forde. AFRICAN SYSTEMS OF KINSHIP AND MARRIAGE. New York: Oxford University Press, 1950.

Reaburn, Janice A. et al. "Social Determinants in Food Selection." AMERICAN DIETETIC ASSOCIATION JOURNAL. 74, 1979, pp. 637--645.

Redfield, Robert, THE LITTLE COMMUNITY AND PEASANT SOCIETY AND CULTURE. Chicago: The University of Chicago Press, 1956.

Ross, Jack C. and Raymond H. Wheeler. BLACK BELONGING. Westport: Greenwood Publishing Co., 1971.

Scanzoni, John H. THE BLACK FAMILY IN MODERN SOCIETY. Boston: Allyn & Bacon, 1971.

Shimkin, Demitri, et al. "The Black Extended Family: A Basic Rural Institution and A Mechanism of Urban Adaptation," In D. B. Shimkin et al. (eds) THE EXTENDED FAMILY IN BLACK SOCIETIES. The Hague: Mouton Publishers, 1978.

Smith, M. G. KINSHIP AND COMMUNITY IN CARRIACOU. New Haven: Yale University Press, 1962.

Smith, Raymond T. THE NEGRO FAMILY IN BRITISH GUIANA. New York: Grove Press, 1956.

Stack, Carol B. ALL OUR KIN. New York: Harper & Row, Publishers, 1974.

Staples, Robert. "The Myth of the Black Matriarchy," in D.Y. Wilkinson and R. L. Taylor (eds) THE BLACK MALE IN AMERICA. Chicago: Nelson Hall Publishers, 1977.

Steelman, Virginia. "Attitudes Toward Food as Indicators of Subcultural Value Systems." HOME ECONOMICS RESEARCH JOURNAL. 5, 1976, pp. 21-32.

The First Congregational Church. 100 YEARS FOR CHRIST, 1867--1967. Atlanta: First Congregational Church, 1967.

Tilly, Charles, Wagner D. Jackson and Barry Kay. RACE AND RESIDENCE IN WILMINGTON, DELAWARE. New York: Columbia University, 1965.

Thompson, Robert A. et al., "Atlanta and Birmingham: A Comparative Study in Negro Housing." In STUDIES IN HOUSING AND MINORITY GROUPS. Nathan Glazer and Davis McEntire (eds), Berkeley and Los Angeles: University of California Press, 1960, pp. 13-83.

Tumin, Melvin. SOCIAL STRATIFICATION. Englewood Cliffs: Prentice Hall, 1969.

U.S. Civil Rights Commission. HOUSING. Washington: Government Printing Office, 1961.

U.S. Department of Labor. THE ATLANTA URBAN EMPLOYMENT SURVEY, July, 1968 - June, 1969. Atlanta: Bureau of Labor Statistics, 1969.

Wheeler, Madeleine and Sanober Q. Haider. "Buying and Food Preparation Patterns of Ghetto Blacks and Hispanics in Brooklyn." JOURNAL OF THE AMERICAN DIETETIC ASSOCIATION. 75, 1979, pp. 560-563.

Wilkinson, Doris Y. and Ronald L. Taylor (eds). THE BLACK MALE IN AMERICA. Chicago: Nelson Hall Publishers, 1977.

Willie, Charles V. A NEW LOOK AT BLACK FAMILIES. Bayside: General Hall Publishers, 1976.

Woofter, T. J. BLACK YEOMANRY. New York: Henry Holt and Co., 1930.

Young, Michael and Peter Willmott. FAMILY AND KINSHIP IN EAST LONDON. London: Routledge and Kegan Paul, 1957.

Young, Virginia Hayer. "Family and Childhood in A Southern Negro Community." AMERICAN ANTHROPOLOGIST. 72, 1970, pp. 269-287.

ABOUT THE AUTHOR

Annie S. Barnes, Professor of Anthropology and Sociology, at Norfolk State University in Norfolk, Virginia, received her Ph.D. degree in anthropology from the University of Virginia, 1971. Dr. Barnes is one of the few scholars who has done extensive ethnographic research on the Black middle class family. Her major publications include "Negro Residential Patterns in Atlanta, Georgia, 1860-1983, and Their Impact on Public School Mixing" (1983), "Black Husbands and Wives: An Assessment of Marital Roles in A Middle Class Neighborhood" (1983), "Twelve to Eighteen Years Old" (1983), The Black Kinship System" (1981), "The Osudoku: Kinship, Political, and Ceremonial Systems" (1980), and "An Urban Black Voluntary Association" (1979).

LIBRARY
ST. LOUIS COMMUNITY COLLEGE
AT FLORISSANT VALLEY.